The Deceitful Sister-in-Law

CHERYL BOWYER

Fulton Books
Meadville, PA

Published by Fulton Books 2024

ISBN 979-8-89221-146-8 (paperback)
ISBN 979-8-89221-147-5 (digital)

Printed in the United States of America

To my love, my children (who are my world), my late father, and my late loving mother. To my late grandparents, also to my aunt and uncle, my siblings, nieces and nephews, cousins, and friends.

A special thanks to my best friends. Thank you all for believing in me and for the unconditional love you show me. I am very blessed to have such a large family and so many friends.

For without all of you beside me, life would just be an empty shell; and with you, I feel you all complete me. I love all of you.

CHAPTER 1

The Beginning

It was a warm spring in 1979 when a baby girl named Katie was born to two loving parents named Lauren and Phillip.

Katie had grown up with kind parents, siblings, and relatives who taught her how to love, be wise, and use strong survival skills.

It was a different time in the late seventies when families raised children and learned to survive. In the seventies, if you were not born into wealthier families, then you had to work your hardest and put your brain skills to the test to have a better life.

Katie was the third youngest of eight children.

Katie was born smart, grew up with a heart full of love, and loved to be useful.

Katie and her family relied on their family farm for food and sold their harvest to meet their winter bills year after year.

Katie loved her young life, and her family was the most important in her life.

Katie made her schooling her top priority, given that her parents had always pushed her to do great and achieve great success in life.

Katie was always a bookworm; in her spare time, her nose was always found in a book.

She also loved helping her parents and grandparents at their family farm after school.

Katie would hurry home from school and quickly finish her studies, just to be able to help her grandparents at their farm.

Katie was always ambitious, trying to get the most out of her time since she was young.

Katie's mother, Lauren, was kind, just like Katie.

Lauren loved her daughter Katie with all her heart.

Katie's mother had always felt she had an incredibly special bond with her daughter since birth.

Lauren had always shown all eight of her children everlasting love and always made them each feel so important to her.

Lauren would never let a moment go by without letting her children know how much she loved them.

Katie's mother taught her and her siblings since they were young about true love and what it took to be a solid, loving family.

Lauren did her best to teach her children the importance of loving parents and their role in their child's life.

Lauren, being a loving mother, never wanted her children to feel any pain growing up.

Good mothers are always trying to protect their children from harm, Lauren taught her children at a very young age.

Lauren explained to her children that they, too, would fall in love one day and that time would teach them if it was their true love. For love comes in many forms, Lauren taught her children.

Lauren taught her children that one day, when they had families of their own, they would pass the love she had given each of them onto their children.

Katie loved hearing her mother telling her and her siblings how life would be for them one day when they grew up.

For Katie knew that it was just a matter of time before she would be old enough to graduate high school and she would leave the comfort of her parents' home.

Katie would read her romance novels and daydreamed about how her life would be if it were like the fantasy of her books.

Katie would imagine how it would be for her true love to find her one day, d aydreaming about how he would ride in on a white horse, carrying a red rose and declaring his love for her.

Katie knew from having older sisters that her fantasies were just those things she only daydreamed about—given how Katie had seen her older sisters dating and how their dates would drive their parents' cars to court them, picking up her sisters at their parents' home.

Katie continued to allow her imagination to carry her off on her fantasy daydreams in hopes that one day her Prince Charming would come to declare his love for her, and they would marry and live happily ever after.

For Katie, her dream was to live in the bigger city, with mountain views from her backyard, instead of the views of flat farmland she had viewed and worked on every day for as long as she could remember.

As Katie's older siblings began to marry and had families of their own, Katie could not help but wonder if she would get her dream, too, one day.

As Katie approached her senior year in high school, Katie's sisters insisted on setting her up on dates.

Since Katie was more into being a bookworm and not so worried about dating, Katie kept telling her older sisters no.

Because her older sisters were persistent, changing Katie's mind, Katie gave in to them.

Katie told her older sisters, "Okay, I'll try dating," to see what all the fuss was about.

Lauren felt that since her daughter Katie was getting older, she wanted her to be more focused on her education, rather than dating.

Lauren knew that her older daughters would not stop trying to get their younger sister Katie experienced in the dating world.

Lauren told Katie that she would rather she wait on dating but decided to go ahead with giving Katie her blessing to start dating.

Lauren felt this was not the right journey for her daughter Katie to take just yet.

Lauren had hoped that once Katie saw what the dating experience was all about, she would continue to focus on her education.

For Lauren wanted all her children to experience what achieving a great education could do for their lives.

When Lauren's older children grew up, they found themselves with families of their own, and their education took to the back seat as their family obligations took the front.

Katie had plans for college and to become successful one day.

Katie was headstrong, and she knew what she wanted in her life. Katie was determined to have her dreams.

Katie wanted to please her older sisters, as younger sisters tend to do.

As Katie found the courage to try dating, she began going on short dates with high school guys that lived locally to her family.

Though Katie had fun, she still did not understand what the fuss of dating was all about. Katie felt she could be just as happy reading one of her favorite books.

Lauren loved this about her daughter Katie, that she was easy-going and high-spirited.

As time went on, Katie became best friends with a senior named Hayden, who had attended high school with her.

Katie and Hayden began hanging out around their neighborhood after school often. Katie was happy to have a close friend.

Katie was pleased that Hayden had gotten along so well with her siblings, especially her younger brother Joey who had looked up to Katie.

Though when Katie introduced Hayden to her parents, they were not incredibly pleased to meet him.

Lauren told Katie, she felt that Hayden was trouble and that he would only wreck Katie's life if he got any closer to her.

Lauren had hoped her instincts were wrong about the young man, but she only knew from her own experience growing up how the bad boy act would surely lead.

For Hayden had come from a different type of family—a family that had values unlike those of Katie's family's values.

Hayden's family values had given Lauren the right to be concerned for her daughter and her daughter's future.

Hayden had all the signs of being a rebel child, and Lauren knew these signs all too well. Though Katie's father, Phillip, was welcoming of Hayden. Phillip had told Lauren to give the young man a chance.

Lauren agreed with her husband to give Hayden a chance, though it was against her better judgment and only to make her husband happy.

Lauren felt that she had to allow her daughter Katie to grow up and make her own choices in life. Lauren had to allow Katie to make her own mistakes, if this was to be one.

As hard as it was for Lauren to let go, she knew she had to let her daughter grow up and hoped she had taught her all the right lessons she could in her young life.

Katie could not help how she felt being around Hayden. Hayden always knew the right thing to say and how to act accordingly.

With Hayden being best friends with Katie's younger brother Joey, Katie felt sure this was meant to be.

Katie had never experienced being in love before; this was her first-time experiencing love.

Katie began wondering if this could be real love—the kind of love her mother, Lauren, had taught her about as a young girl.

As Katie and Hayden graduated from high school, their relationship grew stronger.

Before Katie knew it, Hayden was confessing he was in love with her.

Katie, still unsure if this was real love, allowed her young heart to lead her down a path she had never known. She hoped that she was taking the right pathway for her journey. Katie's head had been hitting her heart, and she felt confused about the path to take.

Lauren grew concerned and tried her best to stir her daughter Katie in a different direction.

Lauren warned Katie that Hayden would only break her heart should she stay beside him and that her life plans would surely change.

But Katie, feeling confused, chose to go with her heart and ignored the warning signs her head were showing would happen should she stay with Hayden.

Against her mother's wishes for Katie to stay away from Hayden, Katie felt following her heart was the right thing to do.

Katie felt that she was living in a real-life romance novel with Hayden. Katie didn't want to dismiss her mother's concerns, but she was young and thought she found true love.

Not long after Katie had turned eighteen, Hayden turned twenty and proposed to Katie asking her to marry him.

Hayden had asked for Katie's parents' permission to marry their daughter.

Her father approved. But her mother denied Hayden the permission to marry her daughter.

Lauren felt her daughter deserved more than what Hayden could give her.

Lauren told Hayden that he would only destroy her daughter's life if she had given him permission to marry her daughter.

Hayden dismissed Lauren's comments and continued with his plans to marry Katie. What Katie would not see in the present time, Lauren's concerns would prove to be right, and Hayden would destroy her daughter, shattering Katie's heart and breaking her spirit.

Though nervous, Hayden still went forward with his plan and purchased an engagement ring for Katie.

Katie felt torn, for her mother had not given him her blessing nor had the proposal been nothing like Katie had dreamed of.

Katie had always felt that her true love would take a knee, and it would be a romantic scene, and he would have her mother's approval. Hayden had done none of these things.

Though Katie's head was hitting her heart once more, she agreed to marry Hayden.

Katie hoped that she made the right decision and that her marriage would have happiness and that her mother, Lauren, would come to accept him the way she did.

Katie allowed her life to move forward.

As time went on, Katie and Hayden began their family.

Katie and Hayden welcomed a son named Kayden into the world.

He was a healthy baby boy, beautiful as all could see. Katie felt her heart would burst from all the joy she felt holding her newborn baby.

As Katie's parents and siblings came to welcome the newborn baby into the world, Katie could not help but smile.

Katie's heart filled with joy as she watched her mother holding her newborn grandson for the first time.

Lauren looked up at Katie and Hayden and said, "You two did great!"

"Kayden is beautiful! My beautiful little grandson," Lauren stated.

Lauren continued, responding to how Kayden looked just like Katie's father when he had been born.

Katie's heart fluttered with such happiness seeing her mother so happy.

As time went on, the family continued bonding and growing together.

Katie continued her education in college and graduated with a degree in the medical field.

Katie always had a love for caring for people. Katie loved helping cure sick patients and helping those in need.

Katie had taken a career working for a medical clinic she had interned for in college.

Katie wanted to make sure she gave her family the best life she could.

As time continued, Katie and Hayden became financially successful. They decided to add another addition to their family and have another child.

Katie and Hayden wanted nothing more than to give Kayden a brother or a sister to grow up with.

It was not long after when Katie and Hayden announced to their families that they were expecting another son later that next spring.

When spring rolled around, Katie had given birth to another beautiful baby boy named Liam.

Liam was just as precious as his older brother, Kayden.

Katie did not think her heart could feel so much love and joy as she held her new baby boy for the first time.

Liam's eyes were as blue as the sea, and he looked just as beautiful as his older brother.

Katie felt as if her life was complete. She felt like she could not ask for more.

As the family came to welcome the new addition, Katie's heart just melted.

Seeing so many of her loved ones there for her and her family, Katie felt very blessed.

Katie could not wait to see what more life had in store for her and her family. Katie felt very excited for her life journey with her family.

As life continued, Katie's family continued to grow.

Her siblings began having more children, giving their parents many grandchildren.

Katie welcomed many nieces and nephews into their ever-growing family.

Lauren felt that she was ever so blessed with so many grandchildren. Lauren felt her life was pure and God's love was strong, giving her so many little hearts to love and spoil.

As Katie's career progressed and her sons began to grow older, Katie felt that her life was going great.

Hayden was adjusting well to fatherhood and getting along better with Katie's mother, Lauren.

Though Lauren had hoped that Hayden would try to do more for his family by continuing his education for a higher-paying occupation, Hayden had different plans for his life moving forward.

Hayden had been working in a factory straight out of high school. Though his family pushed him to go further, Hayden had no intentions of continuing his schooling.

Hayden had come from a family that loved to drink and party. Though his mother and grandmother pushed Hayden to achieve better in his life and to do better than his father and his uncles, Hayden had chosen to follow the same path as the men in his family.

Katie had hopes that with the birth of their two sons, Hayden would see that as a reason to do better in life and continue his education further.

Katie had encouraged Hayden to attend a trade school or find another occupation that would bring him more happiness.

Katie felt that her husband had been going through something in his life.

Katie felt that if she had encouraged him to do better, then he would take the encouragement and find what made him happier.

Hayden was not happy with his occupation, and Katie knew he could do a lot better.

As time went on, Hayden decided to stay at the factory he had worked at for years. Hayden felt there was no reason for him to change his occupation, and he felt further education wasn't for him.

As Kayden and Liam continued to get a little bit older, Katie and Hayden had been blessed yet again with another pregnancy.

As they were excited, to be announcing to their families, they were expecting another baby to be born early the next year.

Lauren was overly excited to hear this great news.

Lauren always knew that Katie always wanted a large family. Having three children seemed to be the perfect amount for Katie and Hayden.

Kayden and Liam were super happy to hear they were getting a new baby brother or sister not long after that Christmas. They were excited about their new sibling arrival and knew they could teach the new baby all there was to know, as big brothers do.

As time went on and Katie's due date arrived, Katie and Hayden announced the arrival of their newborn son named Cody.

Cody was born smaller than his brothers but healthy and just as beautiful as they were.

Katie could not help but cry tears of joy for the love she felt so strongly for her three sons.

Katie's heart overflowed with love and joy as she held her three sons in her arms.

As Kayden and Liam greeted their newborn brother Cody and kissed him softly on his newborn head. They whispered "We're your big brothers, and we'll teach you everything."

As Cody let out a newborn cry, Kayden and Liam smiled at their mother with pride.

Katie's and Hayden's families gathered once more at the hospital to welcome the precious newborn child.

They hugged Katie and patted Hayden on the back to give them congratulations once more.

As time went by, Katie and Hayden settled in at home with their new addition, making them a family of five.

Katie could not have been happier. Katie felt her life was complete, and moving forward would be all about making sure she raised a healthy and happy family.

As time went on and Katie went back to work, Katie's mother, Lauren, and her mother-in-law, Jennifer, helped Katie and Hayden with caring for the children.

Lauren and Jennifer felt they could bond with their grandsons this way, and it would help save the family financially without having childcare costs.

Katie was ever so thankful to both mothers for the help they offered helping with their children.

Though as time went on, Katie noticed a change in her husband, Hayden.

For when Cody had just turned three months old, Hayden had begun to start drinking heavily.

Katie became concerned about this as she knew how Hayden's family had been, and she didn't want him turning out like them.

Katie started noticing how her husband was coming home from work late every day and then coming home drunk.

She was alarmed and addressed the situation quickly.

Hayden did not seem to care for Katie's concerns.

Hayden just knew that he liked how the alcohol made him feel. Hayden felt that it took away any worries he had about life.

Katie had grown more concerned about her husband's well-being and her well-being and her children's safety.

She had decided to take the children and visit her mother, Lauren, for guidance on how to help talk to her husband about his drinking.

Lauren was alarmed to hear this terrible news about Hayden's drinking.

Lauren knew this herself all too well, the harm of drinking heavy, and seeing how Hayden's family was with their partying.

Lauren feared the worst as her concerns were becoming a reality.

Lauren reached out to Jennifer, Hayden's mother, hoping she may be able to assist with the situation.

But Jennifer knew the signs she was seeing with Hayden all too well.

For Jennifer had gone through this situation in the past with Hayden's father.

As Jennifer made a visit to her son's home, she reached out to her son, Hayden, with concern.

Jennifer tried to talk to him and get to the reason for his drinking.

Hayden responded to his mother, saying it was his life and that he would live it how he chooses.

Jennifer reminded her son that he was a father of three precious sons and a husband to a beautiful wife and that he would lose everything if he did not quit his foolishness with his drinking.

But Hayden just turned his back on his mother, telling her to leave his home and that his family was none of her concern.

As Jennifer began to walk away, she opened the front door to leave but paused for a moment and then turned and told her son she loved him. She then pleaded one last time with him to quit his drinking before it was too late.

Jennifer assured her son that she wanted to help him before he loses everything.

Hayden cursed at his mother, told her to get out now, and slammed the door in her face, leaving his mother standing on his porch with tears rolling down her face.

Hayden just grabbed the bottle he had sitting on his table and began to drink it away.

As Jennifer, returned to her home, she contacted Lauren with despair in her voice, saying, "I do not know what to do. I have tried."

Lauren responded that she would keep Katie and their grandsons in her home for safety and that she would pray for a better outcome in the future.

As the next day arrived, Katie had to go to work.

Lauren had agreed to care for her children and assured her they would be okay.

As Katie arrived at her work and began her day, she could not help but worry about her husband's drinking and well-being.

Katie knew that she could not live her life like this. And she would not have her children growing up with a drunken father.

Katie had planned to talk with her husband after work.

Katie arranged for her mother to care for her children after she got off work so that she could try and help her husband see the dangers of his ways.

As Katie arrived at her home, she was surprised to see that Hayden was already home.

Katie had not been expecting him for another couple of hours. For she thought he would surely still be working his factory job.

As Katie made her way to her front door, she was surprised to find the door open.

As Katie went inside, she found Hayden lying on the couch with several empty containers all around him and all over the coffee table and the floor.

As she looked around the room, she could see that Hayden had never left for his shift.

Hayden had been drunk for hours and passed out, not even bothering to shower.

Katie began having tears of sadness running down her cheeks, knowing that her world was falling apart.

Katie began worrying more. She did not want this for her or her children.

Katie wanted things to change. She needed them to change badly.

Katie decided to try and wake Hayden, telling him they needed to talk.

Hayden shrugged her away and turned over facing the couch.

Katie sighed and then said, "Please, Hayden, we need to talk."

Hayden refused to listen to reason and lay there pretending to be sleeping.

Katie began cleaning up the mess Hayden made in the living room. She grabbed a trash bag from the kitchen and began picking up the empty containers.

As Hayden sat up on the couch, he rubbed his bloodshot eyes to clear his vision and yelled at Katie to just leave it.

Katie paused and looked at him.

Hayden yelled once again, "Just leave the damn garbage alone!"

Katie looked at him and said, "Why are you doing this? This is our home. This is our children's home. Why, Hayden? Why are you doing this to us?"

Hayden just sat there in silence for a moment, then began to speak, saying, "This is who I am, who I will always be."

Katie pleaded with her husband to stop this nonsense. Katie told him he needed to get treatment for his drinking problem and that he needed to be sober for work.

Hayden just laughed at Katie and told her he had been fired, that he no longer had to worry about working.

Shocked, Katie asked Hayden how he could do this to their family.

Hayden told her that her mother warned her about him.

But she only saw him as she wanted to see him, through her rose-tinted glasses.

Hayden continued to tell Katie she did not see the real him.

Katie responded to her husband stating that he wasn't the person he was when they married.

Katie told her husband, "You were a kind and loving person, not this drunk in front of me."

Hayden screamed at Katie to get the hell out.

"Leave me be, you bitch!" he yelled. "Go be with your sons and live your fancy life, you bitch! Leave me to be like my family taught me to be!"

Katie's jaw dropped as she replied to Hayden, "You're drunk. You don't even know what you're saying.

"You don't mean any of this," Katie stated to her husband, Hayden.

Hayden responded to Katie, saying, "Oh, but I do. I should have said it sooner."

Katie had tears running down her cheek as she reached for her purse and her keys.

Katie looked at Hayden and said, "You are pathetic! I cannot believe I ever loved you! I gave you three beautiful children—this is what you have become."

Hayden walked to the refrigerator and took out another cold beer. As he slowly popped the tab open, he said to Katie, "Well, with any luck, they will grow up in the future and be more like you and less like me."

Then he turned his back on Katie as he walked back to the living room and sat there in silence—with foul odor rolling off him, reeking of beer and body odor from not bathing for days—with a shadow of darkness surrounding him as he listened to Katie walk out the door and out of his life forever.

As Katie returned to her car, she quickly started the engine and then grabbed the steering wheel crying, tears rolling down her cheek.

Katie began praying aloud, "Please, God, help me help Hayden. He has lost his way, and our children need their father to be sober."

Katie then slowly put the car in drive and began to pull away. She drove back to her mother's home, where her three children were, and prayed for better days.

Once Katie returned to her mother's home, Lauren rushed out to greet her daughter.

As Katie stepped out of her car and into her mother's arms, her mother hugged her tightly and assured her she would be okay.

Lauren told Katie she would be there for her and her children always and that they would be okay.

Katie's sons rushed out of the house, seeing their mother and grandmother in the driveway.

Katie's sons ran to give their mother and grandmother hugs.

Katie quickly dried her tears; she did not want her sons to see her sadness.

Katie's mother assured her daughter that things will improve in time and for her to just come back home so that she and her father could help their daughter to figure out where to go from there.

Katie agreed with her mother to come back to her parents' home with her children, to allow her parents to help her rebuild her life, and to move forward with her children.

Kayden, the oldest, told his mother it would be okay.

He continued telling his mother that they had one another and they had Grandma and Grandpa. "We have our family. We will be okay."

Liam and Cody smiled and continued hugging their mother.

Katie felt a glimpse of hope as she told her children, "Yes, things will be okay."

Katie and her children returned to her mother's front porch, where Lauren suggested for everyone to go in and have a slice of her homemade apple pie.

"Fresh baked this morning," she shared with them.

Lauren hugged her daughter and assured her this was not the end, telling her daughter God has a bigger plan for all of them and that when the time was right, they would see his bigger plan.

Katie thanked her mother for her words of wisdom and her love."

They continued inside Lauren's home and began enjoying their family time together.

Katie sat there with everyone that was the most important in her life, knowing that her mother was right and that her broken heart would heal in time and that her sons, too, would be all right and that this nightmare would all end when the time was right.

As time passed, Katie and her sons settled back in at her parents' home.

Katie's mother loved having her daughter and grandsons there every day, and the memories created were just priceless for the whole family.

Katie told her sons that being back at their grandparents' home would only be temporary.

But her sons had hoped to make it more permanent.

They loved being with their grandparents and seeing their mother so happy.

As the seasons changed, Katie filed for divorce from Hayden.

It had been a long time since she had seen him, nor had he tried to see their children.

The divorce was over quickly, and the judge granted Katie full custody of her children.

Katie could not understand how a father's love could be so empty.

As Katie looked at her precious sons, she felt so much love. She could not understand how anyone could feel anything but love for their children.

As Katie's children grew older, they were surrounded by all their family.

The love the children felt made Katie feel so grateful.

Seeing her sons playing with their cousins, aunts, and uncles made her feel so blessed.

Katie was thankful for her parents and all the help they offered and thankful for her siblings and the support they had given her.

Katie knew she would be okay and that her children would always know how much she loved them. She knew that they would always have their family.

CHAPTER 2

Starting Over

As time passed, Katie and her children adjusted to their new way of life.

Katie continued her career in the medical field, while her sons focused on their schooling.

Lauren stood by Katie, helping her daughter and grandsons as much as she could.

Lauren helped care for the children after school whenever Katie had to work longer than expected.

Lauren loved teaching her grandsons new things.

Lauren taught them how to bake and played their favorite games. Lauren's grandchildren were her pride and joy, just as her children were.

Katie worked hard to make sure her children never went without these growing up and that they still had the little luxuries they enjoyed for their special days.

Katie wanted her children to have a life to be proud of. Even though she was a single parent raising her children, Katie did not want them to feel like it would always be that way.

Katie had taught her children that the good Lord would send the right person for them one day when the time was right. And he would become a part of their family forever.

Katie taught her children that good things come to those that wait and that the time they were in was meant for them to heal and be their own little family.

Lauren was so proud of Katie and of the mother that she became for her three young sons.

Lauren had hoped that the day would come when Katie would meet the right person, who would heal her broken heart, and the right gentleman who would accept her grandchildren as their own sons and make her daughter's world feel complete again.

As time went on and the years passed by, Katie lived her life for her children. Katie wanted to make sure that they grew up right and that they had everything they needed.

Lauren would stay up with Katie night after night after they put her children to bed. They would spend time together talking about the future.

Lauren told her daughter not to give up hope, that the right man for her and her sons was out there, and that when the time was right, he would find her and make her feel complete again.

Katie felt as if she could not think like that, for Hayden had hurt her badly, and she felt as if she could not trust another man again.

Lauren had assured Katie that she could not compare every man to Hayden, that though she picked the wrong apple the first time, the next one would be even sweeter.

Lauren continued telling Katie that the right man for her would know how to treat a lady and know how to be a father to her children.

Katie responded to her mother, saying "I sure hope so, Mother. I sure hope so!" as her mother hugged her and kissed her on the head and then telling her "Trust me, my daughter, you will."

The next day Katie had woken up her children early. It was a gorgeous Saturday morning, and Katie had decided to take her sons out for a mother-and-sons outing.

Katie felt that her family could have an enjoyable time, and what better way to have fun than to go to the zoo.

Katie's children cheered at the idea as their grandma Lauren called out to them, "Have fun, boys! I will see you this evening after work."

The children all waved goodbye to their grandma Lauren and told her they loved her as Lauren prepared to leave for work at the local country diner in town.

Katie packed them a picnic lunch and loaded everyone into the car.

As they headed to the zoo, the laughter that filled the car made Katie's heart fill with joy.

It had been a while since Katie felt that happy, and she took it as a sign that everything would be all right.

Katie kept remembering what her mother had told her: that when the time was right, the right gentleman would find her and be good to her and her children.

Katie felt she just had to hold onto hope that it would happen.

When Katie and her sons arrived at the zoo, they made it a fun-filled day, seeing the animals, taking photos, and enjoying their picnic lunch in the shade under the tree.

Katie could not feel happier seeing her sons enjoying the outing she planned for them.

As Katie watched her three sons feed the animals and enjoy the guided bus tour, Katie smiled with such joy, knowing that she was doing all she could to give them a childhood with many good memories.

As the zoo began to close for the day, Katie and her children headed back home.

As she tucked her children into bed and kissed them on their heads, she was reminded how blessed she was to have three little angels.

Katie felt that if she never found love again, she would still be complete because she had her children; and for her, that is all she needed.

Katie longed to give her children more in life, like a father figure to teach them all the things fathers pass onto their sons.

Katie felt that if she could never give them that, she would always be thankful they had their grandparents and uncles to teach them even more.

The next day, Katie enjoyed her morning coffee with her mother.

Katie told her mother about the amazing time she and her sons had at the zoo.

Lauren smiled, as she was so happy to hear they had such a lovely time.

Lauren told Katie that as time went on, better days lay ahead, and she would feel complete again.

Lauren promised her daughter she would see that her words were true and told her to trust her.

Katie's life routine was caring for her three young sons—Kayden, Liam, and Cody—making sure they were raised healthy and happy, and working her full-time career.

As time went on and the years passed by, her sons grew older.

Katie could not help but long for a life partner—someone she could share her life with and a father figure for her sons, a good man who would love her and her sons unconditionally and treat them with the love and respect they deserved.

Katie decided to start dating casually.

Katie's coworkers had set her up on friendly dates with gentlemen that their husbands had worked with.

Katie, though, could not feel a connection with anyone she had been set up with.

Katie decided to just pause on dating and let the universe take the lead. Katie felt that when the time was right, she would receive a sign from above. Though her mother assured her it was time, Katie felt something had to be missing. She wanted to make sure she got it right this time.

Katie felt that it was important for her and her sons to take things slow.

Katie was looking for a connection to make sure her head and her heart led her on the right path this time around.

The next morning, Katie woke early to find her mother sitting at the breakfast table.

Katie approached her mother saying good morning and poured herself a cup of coffee.

As Katie sat down at the breakfast table to join her mother, Katie noticed a puzzled look on her mother's face.

It was a look Lauren got when she had something to say or even a secret she wanted to share.

Katie smiled at her mother and said, "Mom, what is on your mind?"

Lauren giggled and said, "Whatever do you mean?"

Katie replied, "You know what I mean. You have that look on your face as if you have something to say."

Lauren slowly sat down her coffee cup and looked up at Katie.

Lauren smiled and then began by saying "Well, since you asked, I do have something to share."

Katie began to get curious as it had been a while since she had seen her mother act like this.

As Katie patiently waited for her mother to speak, Katie began to feel nervous. She sensed it had been something about her, and she was eager to hear what her mother had to say.

As her mother began speaking, she talked about her work and how she was constantly happy to see her regular customers at the country diner.

Katie rested her head on her hand as she humbly listened to her mother speaking.

Lauren continued to speak about one of her regular customers that came in every day for his regular meals.

Lauren explained how he was a bachelor that never married nor had children. For he had devoted his life to his career.

Lauren continued to speak about how he always wanted a family of his own, but his career took up most of his time.

With that, he never got around to finding the right person for himself.

Katie smiled at her mother and said, "Oh, Mom, you know I am not looking for anyone right now."

Her mother smiled back at her and said to her daughter, "I think it has been long enough. You know you need to get back out there and find someone."

Katie giggled, as it was not the first time she wondered how it would be to have someone in her life again. Being a single mother, Katie knew it would be hard to find the right person for her and her children.

Being that her children were her entire world, Katie told her mother that though the thought was nice, she could not chance it with her sons.

Her mother smiled at her and said, "Katie, honey, you are a fantastic mother, but you need to trust me. I would not stir you in the wrong direction. I found you the one, the one that you have been waiting for, the one for you and your sons."

As Lauren reached for Katie's hand and gave it a light squeeze, she nodded to her daughter, saying, "Trust me, please. he is the right one. You need to meet him."

As Katie sighed, she said to her mother, "I do not even know the first steps back into this dating game."

Her mother smiled and said, "Leave it all up to me."

Lauren continued by telling Katie, "He already knows a lot about you and is eager to meet you."

Katie looked shocked, wondering what her mother had told this gentleman about her.

Her mother laughed and said, "Now, before you start screeching with questions, know that his name is Dean. He is a good man, honey. He is very polite and comes from good family values."

Lauren continued to tell Katie how she looked at Dean as a friend and that he came into the country diner for dinner every day for his meals, and he was always so kind and had honest eyes.

Lauren continued telling Katie how you could tell a lot about a man from his eyes. Lauren continued telling Katie how Dean was a hardworking man and that he looked after his mother and that since he spent his life devoted to his career, he never found the time to find someone to share his life with.

Katie sat there listening to all her mother had to tell her. She found herself interested in all she had to say.

Her mother continued to describe Dean to her, telling her he was a tall man with dark hair and with eyes as blue as the ocean.

Katie smiled as she began to imagine what he looked like. Katie loved the thought of him having blue eyes, as she and all her children, too, had blue eyes.

Her mother continued to say that he was anxious to meet her, if she were willing, and that she would set everything up.

Katie felt as if it was a little too fast after just hearing about this.

But her mother assured her that Dean was safe and then continued to say, "When was the last time you had a date?"

Which, for Katie, it was forever.

Just then, Katie's oldest son Kayden came into the room. He had been listening as he came down the stairs.

Kayden looked at his mother and said to her, "I think Grandma is right, Mom. I think you need to go on a date."

Lauren smiled at Kayden and said, "See, your son even approves."

As Katie smiled at her son, then back at her mother, she nodded and said, "*Okay*, if your friend Dean would like, I am willing to have a blind date with him."

Katie's mother, Lauren, clapped her hands in approval and said, "Great, I will let him know tonight."

Lauren smiled and then walked away, leaving Katie wondering if she had made the right choice.

C H A P T E R   3

Taking a Leap of Faith

The next day, as Katie went along with her duties of raising her children and doing her career, she could not help but think of the blind date her mother was setting her up on.

Katie wondered if her mother was right and if she had found the perfect man for her.

Katie knew her mother had never approved of her ex-husband, and with her finding Dean, Katie wondered if this was a sign.

As Katie waited for further news from her mother, she tried to stay focused.

Katie did not want things to fall off the path that she worked so hard to keep perfect.

Katie could not help but daydream about how life would be if she had someone new who cared about her and her sons.

Katie longed for someone who'd love her deeply and hold her on those cold, lonely nights.

She longed to meet her soulmate—someone that loved her, someone that would love her sons as if they were their own, and for them to teach her sons all the things that fathers and sons experienced together, the special father and son bond created between two souls.

Katie did not want to get her hopes up though, for she had already been hurt once, and she was not going to allow that to happen to her and her sons again.

Later that day, when Katie returned home from work and greeted her mother and her children, her mother smiled at her and asked her how her day was.

Katie responded to her mother, saying it went well.

Lauren continued, stating that it was good to hear that and that she had some good news.

Katie began to smile and felt a ray of hope come over her.

Lauren began telling her that Dean wanted to take her out that coming weekend on a blind date.

Lauren handed Katie his number and said, "I gave him yours as well."

Katie's heart raced. She did not know how she felt about Dean having her number.

Lauren slowly put her hand on Katie's arm and told her to relax, to take a deep breath, and to know that everything was going to be okay.

She told Katie to trust her, that she did not give her number to a stalker, and that Dean was a good man and he was safe.

Lauren said "trust me, honey, my daughter" to Katie. She said, "I know you've been through enough. You are going to like this man."

Lauren continued telling Katie that Dean had many of the same interests as her and that he has a nice sense of humor.

Lauren continued speaking, telling Katie that that alone was hard to find in a good man nowadays.

Katie began to relax her breathing and said *okay*. She still felt nervous, but she was going to take a leap of faith.

As the week ended, Katie felt more tense about her blind date.

As she tried to plan her perfect date outfit and things to say, her phone began buzzing; Katie had received a new message.

Katie reached for her phone; she was surprised to see the text had been from Dean.

Katie felt her heart racing as she read the message.

Dean had texted saying "hello; I didn't know if you were as nervous as me, so I thought I would reach out to you before our blind date."

Dean continued to say he wanted to make things easier for them, so he sent a text to introduce himself before their first date.

Katie felt that was the sweetest thing ever. As her heart raced with nervousness, she took a breath and responded to Dean, thanking him for his text and introducing herself.

As she texted Dean, she told him it was lovely to hear from him and continued with her introduction.

Katie then continued to tell him that she, too, was nervous about their first date.

Katie told Dean that she found his text welcoming. She thanked him once more for reaching out to her and told him she was excited to meet him. As Dean responded to Katie's messages, they slowly began opening up.

Katie told Dean that her mother had spoken a lot about him. Katie had been looking forward to meeting in person for the first time.

Katie was surprised at how easy it was for her to text Dean.

Dean's responses to her seemed as if she had been talking to a close friend she had known for a while.

After a few dozen texts were exchanged between the two, Katie and Dean agreed to have a meet and greet before they went on an official date.

They both felt that it would be better this way. A casual meetup at the local country restaurant where Katie's mother worked seemed perfect for them.

Katie and Dean had planned to meet the following day.

They both had been free with their schedules and thought it would be a great start to a new day.

Lauren agreed to watch Katie's children while her daughter took some time to have fun.

Lauren knew that this would be the start of something great for Katie, and she knew that Dean was a pleasant man, that he would surely show her daughter a lovely time.

As Katie prepared for her meeting with Dean, she began to feel nervous.

Katie could not help but wonder if he was feeling the same and began to think of some things she would say.

She wanted to make a good first impression and was optimistic that this would turn out great.

Katie trusted her mother's guidance, so she felt this could be the start of something great.

Katie knew her mother would not just set her up with anyone, as Katie and her sons were very important to her.

Lauren wanted someone special for her daughter and her grandsons—someone kind, honest, and loyal and someone that could mentor her grandsons and teach them even more. Although her grandsons had their uncles and grandfather, Lauren felt they needed a father figure.

As the time arrived for Katie to leave for her meet and greet date with Dean, she planned her trip early enough to give herself a few extra minutes and to arrive early at the diner.

Katie wanted to give herself time to take a breath and try and relax her nerves.

As Katie stepped out of her car, she caught the eye of a handsome tall man standing at the diner's entrance.

Katie could not help but feel she knew this man as he began to walk toward her.

Katie suddenly felt frozen, trying to gain the courage to say hello.

The handsome man slowly raised his hand and said, "Hi. You must be Katie. I am Dean."

Katie suddenly felt her heart jump into her throat as she slowly offered her soft hand as she whispered, "Hi, I am Katie."

Dean smiled widely, showing his perfect white teeth and slowly shaking her hand.

He then asked her politely, "May I escort you into the diner."

Katie smiled and replied "I would love that" as she graciously allowed Dean to hold her hand and lead her to their table.

Katie was surprised at how she was feeling meeting Dean face to face.

Dean's face was tan in complexion, and his hair a silky black, and his eyes as blue as the sea.

Katie could not help but catch herself smiling while she sat there with him in their little corner booth, waiting for their server.

Dean was impressed with how lovely Katie looked, getting lost in her blue eyes, with her lips as red as cherries, and her complexion tanned from being kissed by the sun.

Katie's shoulder-length brown hair with her large, wavy curls. All of Katie's qualities had made her ever so beautiful to Dean.

The server slowly approached their table. She politely interrupted and took their order and then excused herself as she politely walked away, promising to return shortly with their meals.

Dean and Katie both began to speak, giggling as they both had tried to speak at the same time.

Katie suggested to Dean to please go first.

As Dean smiled and said *okay*, he started off telling her he hoped she did not mind, but he wanted to let her know how beautiful she looked.

Dean continued telling Katie she was breathtaking.

Katie's heart fluttered with joy as she placed her hand on her heart and whispered, "Oh, you're just too sweet."

Katie thanked him for his compliment and then responded saying you are very handsome as well.

Dean smiled and thanked her for that and then continued to say "your mother underestimated how beautiful you truly are."

Dean continued speaking to Katie, saying "words do not do justice to your beauty."

And Katie began to blush.

They then begin to talk casually about what they did for work and their likes and dislikes.

Dean had told her things that he felt he had not told anyone in years, things that he would only share with his life partner if he had one.

Katie was pleased at how much Dean had shared.

She found herself talking about her dreams and how important her family was to her.

Katie told him many times about how being a mother was one of her greatest blessings and how her sons were her everything.

Dean had told Katie that he admired that about her and that being a good parent first and everything else second was one of the greatest things he admired in a woman.

Dean told her that hearing that from her, he felt a calm come about him, as he was raised by a single mother after his father walked out on them when he was just a senior in high school.

Dean continued telling Katie that he held a special place in his heart for mothers.

A few moments later, their server returned with their meals.

Katie and Dean thanked their server and continued enjoying their meal together.

As they continued their conversation and enjoyed their delicious meals, they felt that they had a connection worth exploring.

Katie and Dean decided to continue seeing each other and explore if there was something more between the two of them.

They felt excited for what the future possibly held for them.

They planned for their first official date the next Saturday as they paid their server and thanked her for her great service and delicious meal.

Dean walked Katie to her car, and Katie thanked him for a lovely time.

Dean responded to Katie, saying "thank you for meeting with me and allowing me to take you on an official date next Saturday."

Dean continued telling Katie he was excited to see her again. Katie smiled and responded to Dean, stating that she was excited to be doing this again too.

First Date

As Saturday morning arrived, Katie felt like a nervous high school girl preparing for prom. It would be the first official date for her and Dean later that evening.

Katie spent the day with her children, creating memories for them to cherish long-term and enjoying everything that motherhood had to offer.

As Katie spent time with her children, she smiled from ear to ear and hummed her favorite tune of happiness.

Katie's children loved seeing their mother so happy, and the feeling that all was well meant everything to Katie.

Katie's children knew that their mother would be going on a date later that evening with Dean, and knowing that their grandma Lauren had set it up for their mother excited them even more.

Katie's mother assured her that the children would have fun while she was out and that she would make sure they were tucked into bed at a decent hour.

Katie smiled, knowing that their grandparents would spoil them while she was out, and she was happy to see her children so excited about it.

As Saturday evening approached, Katie's mother helped her prepare for her date with Dean.

Katie felt butterflies and could not help but have first-date jitters.

Lauren assured Katie it was just her nerves and that she would have a wonderful evening out with Dean.

Katie nodded in understanding to her mother.

As her mother stood behind her, Katie stared into the long mirror in her bedroom, looking at the beautiful dress her mother helped her pick out for her date.

Lauren responded to Katie, saying, "you are so beautiful, my daughter. Just as beautiful as the day you were born."

Katie whispered to her mother, "I love you."

Her mother responded, "I love you more."

As the time arrived for Katie to leave on her official date with Dean, she hugged her children and kissed them lightly on their heads and hugged her mother and thanked her for watching her children for her.

Her mother kissed her forehead and said, "Good luck, my daughter. Remember to enjoy yourself and have an enjoyable time."

As Katie headed out the door and down the walkway to her car. Her mother stared out the door and smiled at her daughter.

Lauren shouted out the door one last time to Katie, saying "Remember, my daughter, you are worthy of love and kindness! Have a wonderful time and drive safely!"

"I love you!" her mother shouted.

Katie waved and responded, "I love you all too."

As Katie arrived at the restaurant, she began feeling nervous once again. The feeling of nervousness began to shadow her as she began to have second thoughts about going forward with the date.

As Katie looked in her rearview mirror to check her makeup before stepping out of her car, she saw Dean pulling up into the restaurant parking lot.

As Katie stepped out of her vehicle and began to proceed to the front of the restaurant, she saw Dean standing at the entrance.

Dean waved and smiled at Katie.

As Katie reached Dean, she told him how nice it was to see him again.

Dean immediately told her how beautiful she looked.

Katie blushed and said thank you and then complimented Dean on how handsome he looked tonight too.

Dean thanked Katie for her compliment and then asked to hold her hand to escort her into the restaurant.

Katie smiled as she reached for Dean's hand, and they slowly walked into the restaurant's entryway.

As the host greeted them saying "welcome," Dean responded with "reservation for two please."

And the host asked them to follow her to their reserved table.

As Katie and Dean settled into their chairs with their romantic candlelit table, the server arrived and asked to take their drink orders.

They smiled, as they both ordered the same drink and giggled, and the server commented, "It is an easy order to remember."

The server walked away to gather their drinks, and Katie and Dean began sitting there like two nervous high school kids on their first date, both shy and not knowing where to begin.

Dean began speaking about how much fun he had with her at the diner doing their meet and greet.

Katie smiled and said she felt the same.

Katie continued telling Dean how the day at the diner stuck with her and that she was looking forward to more fun days like that.

As the server returned with their drinks, she politely took their dinner orders and then responded that it may be a short wait for their meals to arrive at their table.

Their server continued to explain that they had a staff shortage this evening in the kitchen.

Dean and Katie smiled and politely told their server it would be okay.

As the server began to walk away, she turned and told the couple that she would be back with warm rolls to help with their meal wait time.

Dean and Katie smiled and said, "Sounds good, thank you," as they continued their conversation. They began getting lost in each other's eyes romantically.

They were both amazed at the connection they felt between each other. It was as if fireworks were going off outside; the sparks they felt flew.

Katie could not help but get lost in the moment. She could not remember the last time she felt the feeling of sparks.

Katie began to wonder if it was safe to let her walls down and allow herself to start to have feelings for someone again. She reminded herself to continue taking things slowly.

Dean smiled at Katie as though it was painted on his face. His heart felt so full now that he even dreaded the thought of the date ending that evening.

As Dean sat there communicating with Katie and getting lost in her eyes, he could see that she, too, was feeling the same sparks he had felt. Dean was pleased to see this reaction in Katie.

It had been an exceptionally long time since Dean had felt this way.

Like Katie, he hasn't dated for such a long time nor felt a connection with anyone like this.

Dean explained to Katie that he had spent his life focused on his career and caring for his elderly mother.

Dean had thought he found real love once—in high school many years ago. But that was short-lived when his high school sweetheart had chosen to love another, leaving Dean heartbroken and shutting out love and throwing himself into his career.

However, Dean's older sisters assured him he would find true love one day.

Dean put his walls up, fearing he would be hurt again if he allowed another in.

Dean knew that his heart could not bear the pain of another love lost, so he chose to forget true love existed and love his career instead.

Fate had other plans in store for both Katie and Dean though.

Though they both had been hurt by love in the past, love was not done with them yet. Their date was the beginning of something bigger for Katie and Dean. It was the beginning of the rest of their lives together; they didn't know this yet.

As the server returned to their table with their meals, the aroma from their dinner quickly filled the air.

Dean smiled as the server set their meals down, his platter being a large steak and potato in front of him. The server cautioned him that it had been extremely hot.

Katie smiled as she saw the excitement on Dean's face over how happy the dinner had made him.

The server carefully placed Katie's pasta and salad next to her drink and cautioned her that her dinner plate was still very warm.

Dean smiled as he saw how delicious the food looked on Katie's dinner platter. He looked at Katie and said, "A woman after my heart."

Katie giggled as she commented to Dean, "This restaurant always serves the best pasta platters."

The server asked the couple if she could get them anything else. And they replied, "No, thank you."

The server responded with a smile, an "enjoy your meal," and then walked away.

The restaurant continued to fill with customers as Katie and Dean began enjoying their meals.

They could hear the surrounding tables having their conversations and the sounds of them enjoying their meals.

Dean commented to Katie how the restaurant was busy.

As Katie nodded, acknowledging Dean of his observation. As Dean and Katie finished their meals, the server checked in to see if everything was great.

The couple responded how excellent the food and service were and thanked their server.

Their server smiled, thanked them for their patrons, and promised to return with their check shortly.

Dean and Katie continued their conversation as the server walked away.

Katie thanked Dean for such a lovely dinner and his great company.

Dean responded by saying he wanted to thank her for joining him and that it was quite the change having a lovely dinner with a beautiful woman from his everyday routine of eating alone at the local country diner where Lauren, Katie's mother, had worked.

Katie continued by telling Dean she could not remember the last time she enjoyed herself this much on a date.

Katie continued to tell Dean that it was very memorable and that it would stay with her long after that night.

Dean smiled and began to blush.

Katie smiled, seeing that there could definitely be something more coming of this first date.

As the jukebox played country love songs in the background, Katie could not help but feel how perfect this date was.

The server returned with their check, and the couple paid their bill, making sure to tip the server for her excellent service.

The server smiled at the couple as they began to leave their table, and she thanked them again for coming and thanked them for her large tip.

Katie and Dean smiled back at the server, thanking her once more for their wonderful service.

As Dean escorted Katie to her vehicle, she thanked him again for such a wonderful evening.

However, the evening was still early, and neither was ready for their date to end.

As Katie thanked Dean one last time for a lovely evening, he asked if he could give her a hug, fearing it was too soon to ask for a goodnight kiss.

Katie responded with a smile, stating she would love a hug.

As Dean leaned in and hugged Katie, they slowly released from their hug and stared in each other's eyes.

Neither wanting to say good night yet, Dean quickly asked Katie if she would accompany him a little longer on their date and see a movie with him.

Katie smiled with excitement and responded to Dean, telling him she would love to but she needed to check in with her mother and see how her children were doing first.

Katie needed to see if it would be okay with her mother if she would be okay to watch her children a little longer, making sure it wouldn't be a burden on her mother for her to continue to stay out a little longer on their date.

Katie didn't want to burden her mother with all the help she had already given her with helping to babysit her children.

Dean told Katie of course. He said he would wait for her to check in on her children, and if she needed to go home, he would understand.

Dean continued telling Katie he knew her children were the most important to her, and he respected that.

Katie thanked him, then excused herself to call her mother.

As Katie called her mother, Lauren answered and was excited to hear from her daughter.

Katie had asked about her children, and Lauren responded that they were having a wonderful time.

Lauren told Katie that the children were going to take their baths and would be in bed soon.

Katie thanked her mother again for looking after them for her while she went on her date.

Katie told her mother she was having such a lovely time.

Her mother told her she was so happy to hear that and that she knew that this date would be good for her.

Katie told her how Dean asked her to join him for a little longer for a short movie while they were still on their date.

Lauren responded quickly to Katie, saying "Go, my daughter, have an enjoyable time."

Lauren told Katie the children were great and there was nothing to worry about at home.

Lauren told her daughter to enjoy herself and have fun and that she deserved it.

Lauren continued telling Katie that she and Dean needed to get to know each other. She assured her daughter this was the start of something great.

Katie thanked her mother and told her she loved her, then asked her to please put her children on the phone.

As Katie's sons got on the phone, she told them she loved them and that she would be home late that evening so they should listen to their grandmother and behave.

Katie's children responded they would and that they loved her too.

As Katie hung up the phone, she turned to Dean and smiled.

Dean asked if everything was okay.

Katie said everything was great and that she would love to join him for a movie.

Dean said "wonderful" and asked her if she would be okay following him to the local theatre.

Katie responded yes, as they turned and got into their cars.

Dean made sure to drive carefully, ensuring Katie could follow him to the right location.

They were only minutes away, making the arrival quick. As they arrived at the theatre, Dean had Katie park right beside him.

He then asked to hold her hand to escort her into the theatre.

As Katie and Dean walked hand in hand and reached the ticket counter, the clerk asked which show they would like to see.

Dean turned to Katie and allowed her to pick, knowing that she would choose a love story. Dean did not mind; he wanted to make this a date they would always remember.

As Katie looked at the posters and saw that her favorite movie, *The Notebook*, was playing, she said, "This one please!"

Dean smiled and said "of course" to Katie, then asked the clerk for two tickets for the chosen movie.

Once they received their tickets, they continued to the concession stand. They had chosen to share a large popcorn container and purchased two large drinks.

As they made their way to their seats and prepared for the movie to begin, they could not help but feel like they were again in high school.

Dean reached for Katie's hand to hold during the movie.

Katie felt the butterflies in her stomach as the movie began and had her hand in Dean's hand.

Dean smiled at the sight of Katie looking so happy. He knew he could not let the feeling he felt end with this date.

Dean felt it was a connection he had never felt before as an adult. He hadn't felt this way since his first love in high school. Dean could see that Katie felt how strong the feeling was too.

Dean knew this was no ordinary date he was on. Dean began wondering if this was a sign—a sign to let his walls down and let Katie in.

Dean felt that, by the end of the evening, the universe would surely show him more.

Dean felt that this had to be the start of something amazing. As he sat there enjoying Katie's company watching the movie, he allowed himself to get comfortable.

Dean could not remember the last time he felt at peace like he did. Dean just knew that this was something worth exploring, and he hoped by the end of the evening that Katie would feel the same.

As the evening continued, the movie ended.

Katie turned to Dean and smiled.

Katie's eyes were teary-eyed as she always cried with this movie.

Katie told Dean she just loved a happy ending.

Dean handed Katie a tissue and said he loved that she allowed a movie to make her feel that way.

As they gathered their things, they made their way to the exit door and walked back to their vehicles.

Katie thanked Dean again for such a wonderful time.

Dean smiled and told her that he was the one that needed to thank her.

For he could not remember the last time he had had an enjoyable time like he did.

Dean then asked Katie if it was okay to give her another hug good night.

Katie smiled and said she would really like that.

As the couple stood by their vehicles hugging, they could feel the sparks flying yet again.

Katie pulled back and told Dean it was getting late and that she needed to get home to her children.

Dean smiled and told her he understood.

Dean continued telling Katie to drive safely as he opened her car door and helped her into the driver's seat.

Katie smiled and thanked Dean once more and then told Dean to have a good night and to drive safely as she pulled away.

CHAPTER 5

Learning to Trust Again

The next morning, Katie awoke feeling overly excited.

Her parents and her children were waiting for her in the kitchen. Their faces were full of smiles as they waited for news about her date.

Katie's mother, Lauren, could see on her daughter's face that everything went great and that another date was sure to come.

Lauren could not help but be excited about her daughter's happiness.

Katie greeted her family and kissed her children on their heads, then hugged her mother and father and thanked her mother again for caring for her children while she went on her date.

As Katie poured herself a cup of coffee, her mother waited patiently to hear how the date went.

Katie began telling her mother how she had a wonderful time, that their dinner was excellent, and that the service was great. She said that she and Dean watched her favorite love story *The Notebook*.

Katie continued to tell her mother that Dean was such a gentleman the whole date.

Lauren smiled, as she was pleased to hear this news.

Katie's children began giggling with excitement, asking if she was going to go on another date.

Katie laughed and then asked her children if that would that be okay with them if Dean asked her to go on another date.

The children giggled and said yes as they teased one another with excitement.

Katie's mother smiled and said to her, "You see, my dear daughter, even your children want you happy."

Lauren continued, stating to Katie that this was a good thing. "A good sign that you may have found what you have been searching for."

Katie felt a glimpse of hope come over her.

As Katie and her family finished their breakfast, Katie sat at the breakfast table thinking what if her mother was right. Was the universe trying to tell her something? Was fate stepping in and showing her that true love did exist?

Katie was not ready to let her walls down yet. She still had walls up around her heart, and she still remembered the pain she went through with her divorce from Hayden.

Katie wanted to take things slow this time, and with it being just the first official date with Dean, she did not want to get her hopes up yet.

Katie could not forget how her first love deceived her and hurt her and her children.

Katie made herself and her children a promise that she would never allow another person to hurt them like that ever again. It was a promise she was going to be sure to keep.

As the children went on to start their day with chores and play, Katie decided to have a private conversation with her mother.

Katie told her mother her concerns, and her mother listened and offered her wisdom and advice.

Katie trusted her mother and knew her mother only wanted the best for her and her children.

Katie had promised herself she would take things slow and to see what fate had in store for her and her children.

She used this promise as a compass to help guide her in life.

Later that day, as Katie spent time with her children, she felt as if she was gliding on a feather.

Katie could not remember the last time she felt so light. It was as if the universe was telling her things were getting better.

Katie began seeing life in a whole new way and feeling like she had a guardian angel guiding her.

She always felt that her mother was her guardian angel, and she never wanted to lose that bond she had with her.

For Katie, her children and her family meant everything to her.

Growing up with her siblings, her mother made sure they were all remarkably close and had created many memories for Katie and her siblings to cherish always.

This helped Katie grow into a strong, independent woman and a good mother that she was.

Katie lived to make sure she was the best mother to her children.

Katie made sure to always put her children first in her life, the way her mother always put her and her siblings first when they were children.

As the day continued, Katie enjoyed time with her children and her parents.

As night fell upon them, Katie and her children enjoyed a lovely dinner together with her parents.

As they finished the evening out with a delicious dessert, Lauren's homemade apple pie, the family's favorite dessert.

Katie told her children it was time for their baths and then to brush their teeth before they go to bed.

As the children prepared for bedtime, Katie helped her mother clear the table and clean the dishes.

Her mother smiled at her with such love and told her she loved how good of a mother she was to her sons.

Katie hugged her mother and thanked her for always being the good mother she was.

As the children got into their beds, Katie came to tuck them in.

She kissed each of her sons on their heads and told them she loved them very much.

Each of her children replied "I love you more" to Katie.

Katie smiled and told them "I love you more than words can say" as each of her sons said their prayers and then began drifting off into dream land.

Katie turned on their night lights and slowly closed their bedroom doors as she creeped out into the hallway.

Katie proceeded to her favorite spot on the sofa in the living room.

Her parents had the fireplace going as she listened to the sound of the wood crackling in the fire.

The sounds she heard gave her peace as she unwound from her busy, exciting day with her family.

Katie began to cuddle up on the sofa with her favorite throw and reached for her favorite novel as she found herself daydreaming, thinking about her date with Dean.

Katie began wondering if he thought about her and their date too.

Shortly after her daydream was interrupted by the ringing of her phone.

She leaped quickly to answer it, worried that the ringing would wake her children.

It had been Dean calling to her surprise.

Dean apologized once again for the lateness of his call, for he was nervous about the timeline of calling after their first date.

Dean explained that it was new to him dating again and that he was concerned he would come off too strong and scare her off.

Katie responded with happiness in her voice, stating he was fine and that she was happy to hear from him.

Dean began to explain how he could not stop thinking about their date and how he had not felt a connection with someone in quite a long while.

Dean continued speaking how he felt he had to call her and see if she, too, was feeling even remotely the same way.

Katie felt nervous at first, scared to let her walls down.

Katie didn't know if she was ready to speak about her feelings that openly so soon. But then she felt a comforting feeling come over her, and she felt it was safe to openly speak to Dean.

She continued telling him that she, too, had been thinking about him and that she had felt a bit of a connection and that it may be possible to explore it.

Dean was extremely excited to hear this.

He told Katie she did not know how happy this made him feel.

Dean continued to say this was the best news he had heard in years.

Katie giggled with happiness and assured him that though she was willing to explore the possibility of moving things forward with him, that she wanted to keep things going slow.

She wanted to start out as good friends first and continue dating.

Katie told Dean this would give them adequate time to get to know each other and grow from there.

Dean responded stating that that sounded like a great plan to him and that he was looking forward to really getting to know her and then, one day, getting to know her sons and the rest of her family.

As Katie and Dean began speaking about life in general, they felt as if they had both known each other for years.

They found comfort in how easy it was to talk to each other.

Katie felt as if she had known Dean before—as if he had been a childhood friend she once knew and that he was grown now and came back into her life—even though they both grew up in different cities and never went to the same schools.

Katie could not get past the way she felt talking with Dean. She felt as if they may be star-crossed lovers in their lives.

As they continued talking about their favorite foods and hobbies and movies, time was passing them by.

They had been talking for hours before either one of them knew it.

Katie looked at the time, and she told Dean she better get some sleep and that her children would be up in a few hours.

Dean said he understood and that he, too, better get some rest.

He asked Katie if he could call her again tomorrow.

Katie responded stating she would really like that.

Katie told him if he would like to call after she put the children to bed, then that would work best for her.

Dean told her he looked forward to it and that he could not wait.

As they prepared to hang up, Katie said good night to Dean.

Dean responded to her "good night, my angel" to Katie.

Katie felt her heart skip a beat as she hung up the phone.

Dean's words calling Katie his angel really touched her heart. For no other man had ever said that to her.

Katie's mother always referred to Katie as her angel, but no man ever has.

Katie could not help but feel as if this were a sign from the universe.

Katie did not want to get caught up in his words though.

Katie knew that men had a way of saying words that made women feel weak in the knees, giving men the upper hand to getting what they wanted from a woman.

For many men, this was getting the woman into bed, but there were still good men out there that were passionate and looking for their lifelong partner.

The next day, Katie went through the morning humming a happy tune.

Lauren knew that something was different about her daughter and had asked her daughter to sit and share.

Katie giggled and told her mother in time.

Lauren looked at Katie and said "oh boy, I remember that look" to Katie.

Lauren continued speaking to Katie, telling her daughter, "The way you are feeling, I, too, felt like that before."

Lauren continued, stating to Katie that she felt that way when she first fell in love with Katie's father.

Katie smiled and placed her hand on her mother's shoulder, giving it a light squeeze.

As Katie continued getting her son's breakfast and getting her first cup of morning coffee, she took her seat at the breakfast table with her family.

Katie's father looked up at Katie from his morning newspaper and smiled. He told his daughter, "Just remember take things slow, and when the time is right, I want to meet this man."

Katie smiled back at her dad and nodded, letting him know that she received his message loud and clear.

For Katie's father was only looking to protect his daughter and grandsons from any further heartache and pain.

As evening came and Katie had her motherhood duties taken care of and had tucked her children in their beds, she now proceeded to care for her needs and then retired to the sofa with her favorite throw and novel.

Katie knew it would not be long before Dean would be calling her, so she placed her phone close to her as she began to relax.

Thirty minutes later, as Katie began getting lost in her novel, her phone began to ring.

Katie answered on the first ring so that it would not wake her children.

As Katie said hello, Dean answered, "Well, hi."

Dean continued speaking to Katie, saying that he didn't expect her to answer so quickly.

Katie responded, saying she just wanted to make sure the ringing did not wake up her children.

Dean assured her he understood and stated that he just wanted to tease her for a moment.

Katie giggled and responded she liked his sense of humor.

As they continued their conversation, Dean had told Katie that he wanted to apologize as he did not get the chance during their last phone conversation to ask her out again on another official date.

Dean said they got so caught up talking about everything that he didn't realize until after they hung up that he had not asked her out again.

Dean continued to ask Katie if she would please join him on another official date.

Katie answered with joy in her voice stating that she would love that.

Dean said great and that he could not be more excited.

Dean asked Katie how she felt about bowling.

Katie said she liked bowling, though she was not a very good bowler.

Dean responded to her stating that that was great; he told Katie, "I could teach you if you'll allow me, as I am a great bowler."

Katie felt a warmth come over her and said she would really like that.

Dean said, "Great, I look forward to our date."

He continued to ask when she would be available for their second date.

Katie told him she would need to check with her mother and see when she would be available to babysit her children.

Katie continued telling Dean that Saturday would be great if her mother were available.

Dean responded saying super and that Saturday would also be great for him.

Dean continued telling Katie that he felt that bowling would allow them to let their personalities shine and help the nervousness fade away.

Though Katie was not much of a bowler, she was happy about another outing with Dean.

Katie could not help but feel the excitement coming over her.

Katie felt as if she was finally making progress in her adult life with dating. Katie had spent years watching her siblings making progress in their adult lives with their spouses and with her parents being happily married.

Katie longed for that same connection and prayed that she, too, would find it for herself and her children.

As Katie and Dean continued their conversation into the night, Dean told Katie he felt like he had met an angel meeting her.

Katie thanked him for his sweet words and told him she was only a mother and that she lives her life for her children and Jesus.

Dean continued telling her that it was great to hear, for he loved children, though he never had any of his own. He said he had several nieces and nephews that he looked after from time to time.

Dean told Katie he, too, was a Christian and that he liked hearing that she was as well.

Dean continued telling her he felt they had a lot in common and that the connection he was feeling toward her was something real, and he would like to continue seeing where this was leading them.

Katie agreed with Dean that she, too, felt this was a strong connection and that it felt like something real, and she too would like to continue exploring where this connection would lead them.

As the evening grew late, Katie and Dean had decided to say good night to each other.

Katie promised him that she would be the one to call him the next evening.

Dean said once again "Good night, my sweet angel" to Katie.

Both hung up the phone, feeling like they had just said good night to their soulmate.

As Katie laid the phone down and began to get comfortable on her sofa, she heard the stairs cricking as someone was coming down them.

Katie turned to look, expecting it to be one of her sons looking for a glass of water. She was surprised to see her mother stepping off the last step, coming into the living room to see her.

Katie apologized to her mother, stating she did not mean to wake her talking on the phone.

Lauren assured her she did not wake her.

Lauren stated that she just could not sleep, and that gave her some time to speak to her daughter while everyone else was asleep.

As Lauren spoke to Katie, she learned about Dean asking her out on a second official date.

Lauren placed her hand on her heart and said she felt her prayers had been answered.

Lauren told Katie she did not want anything more for her than to find true love and happiness for her and her sons.

Lauren told Katie that she would be happy to babysit her grandsons on Saturday so that Dean could take her on their bowling date.

Lauren promised Katie she would have a fun time with her grandsons and that Katie would have a fun time with Dean bowling.

Katie thanked her mother for helping her watch her children and told her she loved and appreciated everything she did for her and her children.

Lauren responded to Katie stating that she knew how much her daughter appreciated her and all she did to help her.

Lauren then hugged Katie and told her how much she loved her and her grandsons.

Lauren continued telling Katie she could not be prouder of the woman she raised and the mother Katie had become.

Katie felt her heart so full of love she could not be more blessed, she told her mother.

Lauren smiled as she wiped a happy tear from her cheek.

Lauren then told Katie, "It's getting late. We should really get some sleep."

As Katie and her mother retired to their bedrooms for the night, Katie could not help but lay in her bed with thoughts running through her head.

Katie felt her heart was hitting her head. Katie's heart felt like she was falling in love fast, and her head kept reminding her to take things slow.

Katie knew that she had to keep things at a slow pace. After the pain her first love and the father of her children, Hayden, caused all of them, she had to protect her heart and her children's hearts from another heartache caused by a man.

As Katie said her prayers and prayed for guidance moving forward, she prayed for peace and love for her family and her friends.

Katie prayed for protection from another heartache for her and her children.

As she said amen, she began falling asleep.

The night seemed to pass quickly as the morning light peeked through Katie's bedroom window, waking her for the morning.

As she opened her big blue eyes, Katie could hear her children's laughter downstairs.

As she made her way to the stairs and found them in the living room, Katie greeted her children with a good morning and a smile.

As her sons ran to her, Katie hugged them tightly as they giggled and said they loved her.

Katie responded, "I love you all more."

The children hugged her tighter.

As Katie's mother walked into the living room, Katie greeted her with a good morning and smiled.

Her mother smiled back and said, "Good morning to you as well, my daughter."

Lauren continued telling Katie she had fresh coffee waiting for her and that she had made pancakes for everyone for breakfast.

Katie thanked her mother and told her children, "Let's go and have some of Grandma's famous pancakes."

The children cheered.

Katie and her children sat at the breakfast table with Katie's parents as laughter filled their home.

Their home showed so much love that it showed every second of the day.

As Katie sipped her morning coffee, she saw her mother smiling.

Katie could sense there was something that her mother wanted to share.

Sitting her coffee cup down, Katie looked at her mother and said, "Now, Mother, I know you have a secret to share."

As her mother giggled, Katie's father peeked his head over his morning paper.

Lauren began speaking and said, "Well, actually I do. You see, Dean had called me this morning while you were still asleep."

Katie could feel her jaw drop, and her heart started pounding with nervousness.

Katie said, "*Okay*, what did he say?" Katie was surprised to hear that Dean had called her mother so early and unexpectedly.

Lauren continued speaking, trying to hold in her excitement, stating, "He just wanted to thank me again for introducing you and him. Also, he told me how much he appreciated me for the introduction. Dean said that you were sweet and beautiful, and he could not help but feel he had a connection with you. Dean assured me that he would take things slow with you and that you, too, told him you wanted to take things slow. Also, that he would never break your heart. Dean said that was his promise to me, that he would never break your heart."

Katie could feel her cheeks blushing, and hearing the words Dean had said to her mother made her heart beat with excitement even faster.

Lauren continued telling Katie that she felt he was the right person for her and her sons.

Lauren continued telling her daughter, "I did good finding you this man, introducing you to Dean."

Katie smiled, knowing that her mother was the reason she met Dean.

Katie's father gave a smile and then continued to read his morning paper.

Katie reached for her coffee and began taking another sip and then nodded, saying yes to her mother as they continued finishing their breakfast.

Katie could not help but feel this was another sign from the universe. For she had not expected Dean to reach out to her mother to thank her for the introduction and use such kind words about her.

As the day progressed, Katie and her family went on with their family plans.

Katie could not help but think how things would be overall if Dean were a part of her family.

Katie found herself daydreaming about him playing with her sons and doing all the fun things couples do together and family outings.

As time continued, Katie and her family went about their lives with their careers and responsibilities.

Katie continued with her career and creating memories with her three sons. She enjoyed the time she spent with them.

Katie could not help but see how much her sons had grown. They were growing so quickly.

Katie could still remember the day each of them was born. She felt blessed to be their mother and thanked God every day for the blessing of her three sons.

As Katie enjoyed her time at home with her children and her parents, she just felt a sense of calm and peace come over her.

Katie felt she could not ask for a better life than the one she was blessed with. She was so grateful for all God has given her and her family.

As another nightfall sat in, Katie tucked her children into bed; she began the nightly routine she had with her children.

Once her children were sound asleep, Katie took some time to herself.

She remembered her promise to Dean to call him that evening. Though she initially felt nervous, she found the courage to pick up the phone and call him.

Katie could not help but wonder if he would have excitement in his voice when he answered knowing that it was her.

As Dean answered on the first ring, Katie was surprised.

As Dean said hello with excitement in his voice.

Katie could feel her heart skip a beat. She said hello nervously, then told him she was surprised he answered on the first ring.

Dean said he had been waiting for her call and was too excited to wait for the second ring.

Katie and Dean both began to giggle with excitement. There was a sigh of relief knowing they do not need to be nervous.

Trusting My Heart

As Katie and Dean began their conversation and talked about how their day went, Katie told Dean that her mother agreed to sit with her children Saturday for their official second date.

Dean quickly responded saying that was great.

Dean said he was so looking forward to it. Dean told Katie he would set everything up and that all she would have to do was wear something comfortable for bowling.

Katie responded to Dean stating that everything sounded great and said she was excited for their date.

Dean continued to ask her if it would be okay this time if he would pick her up for their date. Dean continued stating he wanted to court her appropriately if she would allow him.

Katie could feel herself blushing and said she would love that.

Dean responded saying great and that it would give him a chance to formally meet her parents, if that was okay with her.

Though he had already met her mother at the diner, he wanted to make things more formal moving forward.

Katie was extremely excited about this and said she would love for him to meet her parents formally.

Katie knew this would surely please her parents as well.

Katie felt that Dean was going through all this planning and that it said a lot about him.

Katie could not help but feel that if a man were willing to go through all the trouble of planning everything for a special second date, then he would sure be willing to put in the efforts it took to make things work for the long run in their future, should they have one together.

Katie was so pleased with Dean for all his efforts with the second date that she could not wait for the day to come to enjoy her date with him.

As Katie and Dean finished their phone conversation, Katie said good night to Dean.

Dean continued saying "good night, my angel" to Katie, something he had done in their last few phone conversations.

Katie could not help but look forward to hearing those words from Dean.

Katie felt comfort in him calling her his angel. Though they were just starting out, she could not help but feel this would be something he would call her for an exceptionally long time.

After speaking with Dean, Katie felt a ray of happiness come over her.

Katie felt as though she could glide across her living room floor.

Katie felt as though she was riding on a cloud of sunshine and happiness. She found herself singing a soft tune as she climbed the stairs to her sons' bedrooms to check in on them while they slept.

As Katie pulled the covers up on each of her sons, she whispered to each of them one by one, "I love you, my son, to the moon and back" and "Sweet dreams, my child."

Katie quietly made her way down the hallway to her bedroom where she retired to her queen-sized, four-poster bed for the night. As she lay there staring up at the ceiling, looking out her skylights at the stars in the sky, she could not help but wish on a shooting star flying by.

Katie had wished that Dean would be the one that she had been searching for all the years she waited.

Katie asked the universe to please let him be the one.

Though she knew she still had to protect her heart, her head was telling her there was something more here that she needed to explore it.

Katie was surprised with finding herself hoping that Dean was the one she had waited for—her true love that she fantasized about her whole life since she was a teenager.

Katie knew as a teenager that her romance novels were only fantasies and not like the real world of romance.

Katie felt surely that this must be real love that she was feeling, though she didn't want to set herself up to be wrong, if it had turned out to be just friendship love.

The next day, as the morning light peeked in through the windows of Katie's beautiful bedroom, Katie arose from her bed with such happiness.

Katie's family was already awake as Katie made her way downstairs to the kitchen.

Katie greeted her children and her parents with a bright smile and said, "Good morning, everyone," then kissed each of her children on their heads.

Katie's family could tell there was something different about her, as they had not seen this glow she carried about her for quite some time.

As Katie poured herself a cup of hot coffee in her favorite mug, she began humming a joyous tune.

Katie's mother, Lauren, smiled at her and said, "That's a nice tune, Katie."

Lauren continued, stating to Katie it has been a while since she had heard Katie humming such nice tunes like that.

Katie's oldest son, Kayden, spoke up and said that that was her happy tune.

Kayden continued stating that his mom hummed tunes when she has had a good day.

Katie smiled as her cheeks began showing a rosy red color.

Katie's father spoke up and said, "Well, daughter, care to share with the rest of us what makes you so happy this morning?"

Katie answered her father's question in saying "Well, Father, what has gotten me so happy is Dean is taking me on a second official date Saturday."

Katie's father smiled and said, "That is good to hear, sweetheart. Where is he taking you?"

Katie continued answering her father's question, telling her father Dean was taking her bowling and that he also was going to be picking her up there at her parents' home so that he can officially court her and meet both her parents for the first time.

Katie's father, Phillip, responded with saying "Wow, sounds like Dean is a gentleman."

Phillip continued to say that he was looking forward to meeting the man that has his daughter so happy and glowing.

Katie smiled as Lauren walked up to her and hugged her.

Lauren whispered to Katie saying "I knew he would be something special for you. I just knew it in my heart!"

Katie whispered back to her mother saying "Thank you, Mom, thank you!"

Katie's sons were super excited to hear this.

Katie's sons were eager to meet Dean, and they were happy to see their mother as happy as she was.

Katie told her children that she and Dean were starting off as good friends and allowing their friendship to grow from there.

Katie's oldest son, Kayden, loved this idea and felt that there was going to be a lot more happiness and good times coming.

Kayden could not be prouder of his mother.

Katie's two younger sons, Liam and Cody, were thrilled, too, that their mother was so happy.

Katie's children knew that their mother was dating again, and they hoped that one day she would find love again and that they would be a complete family again.

Katie's children wanted nothing more than for their mother to have someone to share her life with and for her to remarry and gain a new father figure in their lives to have the feeling of being complete again.

Katie was very protective of her children and their hearts.

Katie knew that her mother's words of wisdom would prove to be true one day, that she would find real love and happiness as her mother Lauren assured her she would.

Katie patiently waited for the universe to show her signs that this would happen.

As time went on and Saturday grew near, Katie could feel herself getting nervous once again.

Dean would be arriving at her parents' home to court her for their second date and meet her parents for the first time.

Lauren helped Katie prepare for her date and assured her that her children would be fine.

Lauren had planned a fun evening of activities for her grandsons.

Katie's father sat comfortably in his easy chair as they waited for Dean's arrival.

Katie bit her lower lip as she has done at times when she was nervous—a nervous tick she had since she was a child.

Katie was looking forward to her date with Dean.

Though she was not much of a bowler, Katie felt it was going to be a great date. She was eager for the experience the evening would bring to them both.

Moments later, Dean pulled up in the driveway driving his old pickup truck.

Katie's father smiled seeing the truck was an older Chevy.

Katie's father, Phillip, told Katie that Dean definitely has good taste in trucks.

Katie giggled, knowing that her father was a Chevy man.

Dean walked up the walkway and onto the covered front porch, then rang the doorbell.

Katie's mother Lauren answered the door and politely invited Dean inside.

Dean thanked her as he wiped his shoes on the outdoor rug before stepping indoors.

Katie's father stood up from his easy chair and walked to the foyer where Lauren stood with Dean and introduced himself to Dean with a polite greeting, stating as he extended his hand out for Dean to shake it that his name was Phillip and that he was Katie's father and that it was a pleasure to meet him.

Dean shook his hand firmly and said to Katie's father that it was nice to meet him.

Dean continued to thank Phillip for allowing him to come to his home and to take his daughter on a date.

Katie's father smiled and said, "That is a firm hand shake you have there, son. A strong handshake tells a lot about a man."

Phillip continued speaking to Dean, stating that he felt that Dean was good man.

Phillip then complimented Dean's truck, stating that he liked old Chevys.

Dean thanked him and then quickly responded about the big block engine he had in the truck.

Katie's father shook his head in approval and said, "That's my kind of truck."

As Katie walked into the room with a smile and greeted Dean, she noticed Dean's reaction of her was a wow in excitement.

Dean told Katie she looked beautiful.

Katie thanked him for the compliment, then responded to Dean stating she saw he has met her parents officially.

Dean smiled and said, "Yes, I have, and they're very kind with a smile."

Lauren politely interrupted the conversation by asking Dean about the plans he had made for him and Katie for the evening.

Dean responded politely, sharing that he and Katie would be bowling and then have dinner afterward and that they would not be out too late.

Lauren responded, "Sounds lovely, Dean. I'm sure you two will have a great time."

A moment later, Katie's sons came down the stairs.

Katie greeted her sons and then said to her children, "Boys, I would like you to meet a new friend of mine. Boys, this is Dean, the gentleman that your grandmother and I told you about."

As Dean said hello, Katie introduced each one of her sons one by one.

Dean held out his hand, shaking each of their hands one by one.

Kayden, being the oldest son, shook Dean's hand firmly, telling him "It was nice to meet you, sir."

Dean responded to Kayden stating it was nice to meet him as well.

Liam shook his hand secondly and looked up at Dean with wide eyes and said, "Hello, sir. My, you're tall." Dean gave a light laugh.

Dean responded to Liam saying "Hello, young man. It's nice to meet you."

Dean continued playfully stating to Liam that he was so tall cause he ate all his vegetables, and he continued telling Liam if he ate all his vegetables, he would grow up to be tall too.

Katie smiled at Dean and Liam.

Liam replied, "I'll make sure to eat all my vegetables every day, sir," and he gave Dean a smile.

Cody, being the youngest and the shyest, said hello as he peaked his body from behind Katie.

Dean said, "Hello, little man, nice to meet you."

Cody giggled and took off to hide behind the sofa.

Lauren giggled and said to her grandsons, "Well, boys, let's go start our own activities and let your mother and Dean go start their date."

Katie hugged her children and her mother and thanked her parents again for sitting with her children.

Katie's parents told Dean and Katie to drive safe and have fun, as they made their way out the door.

Katie and Dean walked down the steps of the covered porch hand in hand. As they heard the screen door open behind them, they turned to see Kayden looking out the door.

Kayden being Katie's oldest son said to Dean, "Be good to her. She deserves the best."

Dean responded with a smile. "You're right, Kayden, she does, and I promise I will be good to your mother and see that she gets the best."

Kayden smiled and went back inside to join his brothers and grandparents for their activities.

Katie smiled at Dean as Dean commented that she had three really great kids and that he could see how they really love their mother.

Katie thanked Dean and said, "Yes, I have three great kids. I am really blessed. They are my whole world."

As Katie and Dean continued making their way to Dean's truck, Dean opened the passenger door for Katie and helped her inside and then jumped in the driver's side. They pulled out of the driveway of Katie's parents and made the short drive to the bowling alley."

As Katie and Dean arrived at the bowling alley, Dean politely opened the door of the truck and helped Katie out of it.

Dean asked for Katie's hand as he escorted her to the entrance of the bowling alley.

Katie could feel her heart racing with happiness as they went inside.

To Katie's surprise, the place was not too busy, and everyone was so polite.

Katie and Dean approached the counter to pay for their bowling shoes and the lanes used to play the game.

Dean smiled at Katie and told her, "Don't be so nervous." Dean promised Katie it would be a fun date.

Katie felt a calming sense come over her as she followed Dean to their lane.

Katie politely reminded Dean that she was not too good of a bowler.

Dean quickly responded with kindness saying that it was okay and that it was all about having fun.

Dean told Katie that he could teach her if she would allow him to help her.

Katie responded smiling, stating that she would love that.

As they began their game, Dean took first play, as he knocked the pins down and yelled "Strike!" with a smile on his face.

Katie blushed and said giggling, "You have me beat already!"

Dean responded to Katie with laughter in his voice. "Your turn. Just take your time, and remember it's all in the wrist. Remember to have fun!" Dean said smiling.

As Katie took her place and held her ball, she leaned in and gave it a roll.

As she watched it rolling down the lane, she bit her lower lip, a nervous tick she had.

The suspense made Katie so nervous that she decided to cover her eyes; suddenly, she heard laughter as Dean yelled "Strike!"

Katie quickly looked up and giggled in surprise as she has seen she got a strike.

Katie looked at Dean and said "Beginner's luck I guess" with laughter.

Dean smiled and laughed and then stood to take his place on the lane.

As Dean took his turn, he watched the ball rolling down the lane and knocking down all the pins.

Dean yelled with laughter, "Another strike for me!"

And Katie applauded.

Dean turned to her and said, "Now let see you get your second strike."

Katie stood there nervously; she was not sure if her luck would run out.

Katie began to tense up, but then she felt Dean approach her and started to relax.

Dean lightly stood behind her and whispered in her ear, "Let me help you. Will that be okay if I do?"

Katie nodded to say yes.

Dean whispered, "No need to tense. It is just us playing a game. Just a friendly game."

Suddenly, Katie felt herself relaxing again.

As Dean took Katie's arm into his hand and then guided his hand down to her hand, he said, "Now hold your wrist like this," as Dean showed Katie the correct bowling form.

Dean guided her hand and her arm to her side and then helped her take the ball into the appropriate position.

Dean said, "Now gently release the ball onto the lane and watch it roll."

As Katie let go of the ball and watched it roll down the lane, she turned to catch a glimpse of Dean's eyes, and her heart began to flutter with excitement.

Dean shouted with joy, "Strike again!"

Katie turned to see the pins all down, then she turned back to Dean and said, "We did it!"

Katie hugged Dean in excitement.

Dean suddenly surprised her with a passionate kiss—a kiss so passionate that Katie felt her foot pop up, just like in the romance novels she read.

Realizing they got caught up in the moment, Katie pulled back.

As Dean apologized for the surprise kiss, Katie assured him that it was okay and that they got caught up in the moment.

Katie was surprised at how much she liked the passion of the kiss and the connection she felt between them with the kiss.

For Katie, she had not been expecting Dean to surprise her with a passionate kiss like that.

They both had agreed to take things slow, and neither had planned to get caught up in the moment like they had, though Katie knew that no one could control life at every moment.

It was something that her mother taught her at a youthful age.

Dean continued to apologize once more for the surprise passionate kiss.

Katie assured him that everything was fine.

As they finished their bowling date, they turned in their gear, then Dean walked Katie hand in hand back to his truck.

Dean felt he overstepped with the kiss, so he decided to ask her one last time if everything was really okay.

Katie assured him that it was and told him that she felt embarrassed because she honestly enjoyed the kiss.

Katie was surprised at the passion she felt with it.

Katie continued stating that the connection of the kiss was a powerful one.

Dean smiled and said he was sure glad to hear that.

For he, too, felt a powerful connection and liked the excitement over the kiss.

Dean said he knew they agreed to take things slow, and he was worried if he had said anything he would surely scare her off. He didn't want to lose a chance with her.

Katie assured Dean that she was not going anywhere and that they would continue to take things slow.

Dean was happy to hear Katie speak those words. Dean told Katie the last thing he wanted to do was mess things up with her, as it had been a long time since he felt such a connection with anyone.

Dean didn't want to lose Katie, especially before he had a chance to see where this connection they shared was going.

As Katie and Dean finished having their date and the night came to an end, Dean drove Katie home.

As they arrived back at the home of Katie's parents, Dean and Katie sat for a moment in Dean's truck.

They wanted to enjoy the moment just a minute longer before saying good night.

Katie thanked Dean again for such a fun evening and a joyful experience.

Dean thanked her for accepting the invitation and told her he had such a wonderful time and that he would never forget it.

Katie began blushing as Dean asked if he could give her a good night kiss on her check.

Katie said "absolutely" smiling. Her heart began to race as Dean reached over and gave her a light kiss on her cheek.

Dean then stepped out of the truck, walked to the passenger door, and opened it to help Katie get down from her passenger seat.

Dean gently took Katie's hand as he helped her down from the truck.

Katie smiled and thanked him for his kindness.

Dean continued holding Katie's hand as he walked her up the walkway to the covered front porch of her parents' home.

As they stood their hand in hand, Katie thanked Dean once more for a lovely evening.

Katie reached in to give Dean a good night hug, and Dean hugged her with love in his heart.

Katie could feel the warmth in Dean's heart.

As they released from their hug, Dean said to Katie, "Good night, my sweet angel."

Katie smiled and blushed. She said good night and thanked Dean again for a wonderful time as she watched Dean walk back to his truck.

Katie felt herself floating once more.

Dean stopped and turned smiling at Katie one last time before reaching his truck. He said to Katie, "Can I call you tomorrow?"

Katie smiled and said, "I would love nothing more!"

Dean smiled and nodded, saying "Great!"

Dean felt as if he could jump in the air and shout "Yes!" in excitement.

As Katie quietly entered the front door of her parents' home, she stayed as quiet as a mouse.

Everyone was asleep, though her parents left the living room light on as a way for Katie to have safety.

Katie smiled seeing this, knowing she was so loved.

Katie felt very blessed to have such a loving family. She knew she had so much to be grateful for.

CHAPTER 7

The Start of Something Good

The next day, Katie's mother could not wait to hear how her daughter's date went with Dean.

Lauren was so excited when Katie awoke the next morning.

Katie's children and mother were waiting for her as eager as could be at the breakfast table.

Katie greeted everyone by saying "Good morning, family."

She hugged each of her sons one by one and then hugged her parents.

Katie then gathered her favorite mug and began pouring her morning cup of coffee.

Her mother smiled at her and said, "Well, how did it go?"

Katie giggled and said, "Caffeine first please!"

Her children began giggling at the funny faces their grandmother had made at Katie.

Lauren made faces for silliness toward her daughter—something her grandchildren loved to see.

Katie looked up from her mug and said "Okay, okay" with a smile on her face.

She continued telling her family it went great.

Katie's mother, Lauren, spoke up and said, "I knew it. I knew you and Dean would have fun!"

Katie giggled at her mother as her children begin high-fiving one another.

Katie's mother began cheering with excitement as she stood up from the breakfast table and began swaying side to side, doing a little celebratory dance.

Katie was amazed at how happy everyone was about her having a great date.

Katie knew her family longed for something more, and she began feeling as if this could be the start of something even greater.

Katie knew that God had a bigger plan for her and her family.

Katie had no idea that it could be starting with her finding a new partner in life.

As the day went on, Katie could not stop smiling.

Katie could not get Dean off her mind.

Katie never expected to feel this way again. Katie had not felt like this since she married her ex-husband at such an early age.

Katie felt she was beginning to learn the difference between young love and adult love.

Katie only knew now that she was older and matured with wisdom that she had to get love right this time for her and her children's sake.

As the day went on, Katie decided to make it a mom-and-sons' afternoon.

Katie wanted to give them as much of her time that she could with her busy work schedule.

As the afternoon arrived, Katie had decided to take her sons fishing for the afternoon, something they loved to do together.

As Katie and her children enjoyed their time together fishing, they caught several fishes and released them.

Katie cherished every moment she spent with her children, and she could tell they were cherishing the time they spent with her.

As nightfall sat in, Katie and her sons loaded up the fishing gear and drove back to her parents' home.

As Katie returned home with her children after a long afternoon of fishing, her children told their grandparents about all the fish they caught and released.

Their grandparents expressed how great that was to their grandchildren. They told the children to go clean up and get ready for dinner as it would soon be on the dinner table for them.

As the children quickly ran to clean up for dinner, Katie's parents told her they were happy to see that she and the children had such an exciting time fishing.

Katie smiled and responded to her parents that it was definitely a great time with her sons, then she excused herself to clean up for dinner.

As the family sat down at the dinner table, Katie's father said, "Grace over their dinner," and then the family began enjoying a delicious meal Lauren had prepared.

Katie thanked her mother for such a delicious dinner.

Katie's father, Phillip, agreed with Katie that dinner was delicious and thanked his wife, Lauren, for preparing it.

Lauren smiled and thanked them for their compliments.

The sounds of chewing the children made as they enjoyed their dinner showed Lauren that her grandchildren were enjoying the delicious meal too.

As the family finished their meal, Katie and her children began clearing the table and doing the dishes.

Katie's parents had rested in the family room watching their favorite show.

As Katie and her children finished the dishes, the children went off to play in their rooms.

Katie joined her parents in the family room to watch their favorite show with them.

Lauren thanked Katie for clearing the table and doing the dinner dishes.

Katie smiled at her mother and thanked her for cooking and all she done every day for their family.

Lauren squeezed Katie's hand to show her daughter love.

A while later, the show Katie and her parents were watching ended.

Katie excused herself and attended to her children.

Katie tucked her sons into their beds and kissed them each on their heads, telling them she loved them and to have sweet dreams.

As her children responded to her saying "I love you more," then said their prayers and drifted off to dreamland.

Katie turned on their bedside lights and slowly tiptoed out their bedroom doors.

Katie turned and whispered one last time to her children as they slept, telling them she loved them to the moon and back.

Katie made her way down the hallway and back downstairs to join her parents in the family room.

Katie noticed her father had retired to his bedroom. Her mother was still sitting in the family room, rocking in her favorite chair.

Katie took a seat next to her mother, in her father's easy chair, as she let out a sigh of exhaustion from a long, enjoyable day.

Not long after, Katie's phone began to ring, and she reached for it quickly so that it wouldn't wake up her sleeping children and father.

Katie noticed it was Dean. Her heart began to race as she said hello.

Dean greeted her with such excitement in his voice. He told her he hoped it was not too late to be calling.

Katie responded with joy in her voice saying no and that it was fine.

Dean continued speaking telling Katie he just wanted to thank her again for their last date and that he could not get her off his mind.

Katie told Dean she could not get him off her mind either.

Lauren turned and looked at Katie with a smile and whispered to her, "Is that really Dean?"

Katie nodded as Lauren sat patiently with a smile.

Katie and Dean began talking about making plans for another outing.

As Lauren could not help but overhear her daughter's conversation with Dean, Lauren felt excitement come over her.

Lauren politely interrupted her daughter's phone conversation for a moment.

Katie asked Dean if he could please hold for a moment so that she could speak to her mother.

Dean said sure and that he would be there waiting patiently for her to come back on the line.

Katie thanked him and said it would only be a moment.

Katie then turned to her mother and waited to hear what she needed to say.

Lauren told Katie she just wanted to suggest having a family picnic the following weekend and for her to invite Dean.

Lauren insisted that it would be fun and that it would give Dean a chance to get to know her family better and allow him to see how she interacted with her children.

Katie smiled at the idea and told her mother, "Okay, I will ask him if he would like to join us for a family picnic next weekend."

Lauren smiled with excitement as she waited for Dean's response.

As Katie continued her phone conversation with Dean, she politely told him about her mother's idea of a family picnic the following Saturday and asked if he would like to come with them.

Dean immediately responded to Katie saying he would really like that.

Katie, smiling ear to ear, told him, "Great, I will get ahold of you tomorrow with the details."

As they said good night to each other, Dean made sure to sign off with saying "Good night, my angel" to Katie.

And Katie said good night with happiness in her voice.

Lauren, so excited, was eagerly standing by her rocking chair waiting for a response from Katie.

As Katie laid the phone down, Lauren looked at her and said, "Well, what did he say?"

As Katie responded that he accepted the invitation, Lauren began cheering, stating that she would have to make sure she planned the perfect meal for the picnic.

Lauren assured her daughter that it was going to be great as Lauren said good night to her daughter and retired to her bedroom.

Katie stayed a moment longer in the family room.

Katie could not help but feel excited, for her life was beginning to change for the better.

Katie could feel that something good was coming and felt incredibly grateful for all her blessings.

Katie knew that she would not be where she was at in that stage of her life if it had not been for her mother's help and guidance.

As the weekend approached, Katie contacted Dean and gave him the information needed for their plans for the family picnic that Saturday.

Dean was very eager for the picnic and told Katie he could not wait.

Katie and her mother spent many hours planning and preparing for the perfect family picnic with Dean.

Katie was optimistic that things would turn out well.

Katie could feel herself falling increasingly for Dean each day. She reminded herself to take things slow, as she could not go through another heartache.

As the week continued, Lauren helped Katie plan for an exceptional picnic.

Katie reached out to Dean and confirmed with him all the details for the picnic and assured him it would be a fun time.

Dean responded to Katie stating that it sounded like it was going to be a blast and that he couldn't wait to spend more time with her and get to know her family better.

As Saturday arrived, Katie and her children loaded up their car with things needed for the picnic.

Katie's parents loaded their car with extra picnic supplies they felt could be used for more fun on their family outing.

As Katie and her family arrived at the city park for their picnic, they were surprised to see Dean was already there waiting for them.

Dean smiled and waved at them as they pulled into the parking lot. He greeted Katie and her family and helped them unload all the things for the family picnic.

Katie thanked him smiling as she handed things to her sons to carry to their picnic table.

As Katie and her family began setting up at their picnic table, Dean offered to start the grill.

Katie's father responded saying, "I think that would be helpful."

He helped Dean tend to the grill.

Katie and Lauren began preparing everything for their picnic as the children ran and played in the park.

Katie told her sons to be careful and stay together and to be back at the table when they heard their grandmother ring her cowbell for lunch.

The children responded "yes, Mother" as they ran to play on the swings in the park.

Dean looked at Katie and said, "Those are some good boys you have there."

Katie responded by saying "Thank you. They are my entire world."

Dean and Katie's father continued to cook the BBQ on the grill.

The smell of the delicious food had traveled and gotten the attention of Katie's sons.

Shortly after, Lauren began ringing her cowbell she had brought, and Katie's sons came running.

Katie told her children to run and clean their hands quickly as she continued pointing them in the direction of the restrooms north from where the picnic table was located.

Her children ran and quickly cleaned their hands and hurried to return for their picnic.

As the children arrived back at the picnic table, they took their seats and waited patiently as their grandmother and mother prepared their plates.

As Dean and Katie's father, Phillip, sat the pan of BBQ down on the table, they took their seats at the table to join the family for their picnic.

As Katie handed each of her sons their plates, the rest of the family prepared their own.

Katie spoke up and said she would like to thank her parents for helping with the picnic and to thank Dean for joining them.

Katie told her children to please thank their grandparents for helping plan and prepare the picnic and to please thank Dean for coming and for his help with the grilling.

The children all shouted at once, "Thank you, Grandma and Grandpa! Thank you, Dean!"

Everyone giggled and said, "You're welcome, boys."

Then Lauren said, "*Okay*, everyone, let us bow our heads and pray—thank the good Lord for this delicious picnic!"

As they said their prayer and gave thanks, the family said amen.

Katie felt proud that her family was always giving thanks before every meal. She was also proud that Dean felt the same way and took part in giving grace.

As the family had finished their picnic, everyone helped clean up the mess and loaded the dishes and things back into their cars. Katie told her children they were free to play for a while.

Katie's boys decided to sit back at the picnic table with their family.

Cody pulled out his action figures that he brought from home and began playing with them.

Kayden sat there playing with his cell phone that he had gotten for his birthday awhile earlier.

Liam pulled out his drawing pad and colored pencils.

Katie smiled seeing her children wanting to stay at the picnic table with their family.

As Katie and Dean joined her children back at the table, Katie's parents had decided that they would let Katie and Dean enjoy the remainder of the picnic with her sons and that they would return home.

Lauren told Katie to have an enjoyable time and that her and her father would see them all back home later that day.

Katie hugged her parents and thanked them.

Katie's parents told their grandchildren to behave and have fun, and they thanked Dean again with a smile on their faces for joining them.

Katie and Dean enjoyed the rest of the picnic with her sons Cody played with his action figures while Liam began to sketch them.

Kayden played a robot game on his cell phone.

Katie and Dean begin talking to her children.

Katie asked her sons what else they would like to do today on their picnic.

Cody, being the youngest, responded that he just wanted to play with his action figures.

Katie smiled at her sons just as Dean began speaking to Cody about his action figures.

Dean said, "*Wow*, that is a cool action figure. What kind are they?"

Cody looked up at Dean and said, "X-Men, my favorite two."

Dean responded to Cody stating that was awesome.

Dean continued telling Cody, "I used to have some X-Men action figures when I was about your age."

Cody responded to Dean saying how awesome that was.

Just then, Liam laid down his sketch pad and began paying attention to the conversation between Dean and Cody.

As Dean noticed the sketch that Liam had drawn, Dean looked at Liam and said to him that he was quite talented, as the sketch looked just like Cody's action figures.

Liam smiled and thanked Dean and asked if he would like to see the other sketches he had drawn.

Dean responded saying he would really like that.

As Liam began showing him his sketchbook and all his sketches one by one.

Dean told Liam he was quite impressed and that he has a real talent.

Liam thanked Dean for his kindness.

As Dean replied to him stating that he didn't have to thank him and that he really was talented.

Kayden had put away his cell phone and decided to take part in the family discussion.

Dean asked Kayden if he had any hobbies he liked doing or played any sports.

Kayden responded saying how he enjoyed playing basketball in his spare time and that when he was in elementary school, he had played Little League Baseball.

Dean responded to Kayden telling him that it was awesome that he liked playing basketball in his spare time, also how it was even cooler that he played little league in his elementary years.

Kayden smiled at Dean and said maybe they could shoot some hoops sometimes, stating that he had a basketball court at his grandparents' house.

Dean responded to Kayden saying, "Yes, most definitely, if that is okay with your mother and grandparents?"

Katie smiled and said that it would be great.

Kayden's face lit up with joy. He sat there enjoying the warm breeze with his family.

Liam began speaking to Dean, asking if he liked to draw or sketch.

Dean said he liked to, but he was not as talented as Liam was.

Liam smiled and said, "It is okay. If you enjoy doing it, then that is what matters most."

Dean smiled, responding to Liam telling him he was absolutely right.

As the afternoon ended, Katie told her children they better get ready to return home, as it was starting to get close to dinnertime.

Katie and her children said their goodbyes to Dean and thanked him again for the enjoyable time and for joining them on their picnic.

Katie hugged Dean, and then Dean shook the children's hands one by one, thanking them for sharing their fun with him.

Katie and her children loaded into her car, and Dean hopped into his truck. They waved goodbye one last time as they watched Dean pull out of the parking lot first.

Katie followed and then turned in the opposite direction of Dean, heading back to her parents' home.

As Katie drove home, her children were beginning to fall asleep from the fun day they had.

Katie could not help but think about all the excitement and all the cherished memories they had created during the picnic.

Katie knew she would have to thank her mother again when she arrived home.

For her mother had planned the picnic, and if it had not been for her, she would have never met Dean and felt this happy again.

Katie knew she would cherish this moment forever.

CHAPTER 8

Moving Forward

Later that evening after arriving home, Katie had her children clean up and then prepared for dinner before tucking them into bed for the night.

Katie had thanked her parents again for all their help with the picnic and told them she and the boys had a wonderful time.

Katie continued telling her parents that Dean sent his thanks too and that he mentioned he had a great time.

Lauren was so pleased to hear such praise of gratitude from her daughter and Dean.

Lauren felt she knew that if she and Katie's father, Phillip, left the picnic early, it would give Katie and Dean some alone time with the children and that they would have a wonderful time, making it a bonding experience for Katie and Dean and for Dean to get to know Katie's sons better.

Katie could not help but feel her heart was so full of joy. It was as if it would burst from happiness.

After caring for her children for the evening and tucking them into bed, Katie went on with her nightly routine. She could not help but think about all the details of the picnic and wondered what Dean was doing that evening.

Katie decided to give him a call and say thank you one more time before the evening had gotten too late.

As she called Dean, he was quick to answer.

Dean was excited to receive her call.

As Katie told him she wanted to thank him again for joining them on their picnic and how much fun they all had, Dean responded that he, too, had an exciting time and that she had great kids.

Katie thanked him for his compliment and said, "Yes, I am really blessed. They are some amazing kids."

Dean continued the conversation with asking Katie if it would be okay to make plans to come over sometime and play basketball with Kayden.

Dean said he wanted to uphold his word and shoot some hoops with Kayden sometime if that was okay.

Katie said that would be great and that Kayden would love that. She felt this would give her and her two younger children more time to bond with Dean as well.

As Katie and Dean continued their conversation a little longer, the night became late, and they had to say good night.

They promised each other they would talk soon.

As Dean ended the phone conversation, saying "Good night, my angel" to Katie, as he had always done, Katie could feel herself blushing, said good night, and hung up the phone.

As she laid the phone down, she made her way upstairs and retired to her bedroom for the night. Hoping that her dreams would be sweet, she began saying her prayers before falling asleep softly.

As the weeks went on, Katie focused on her career and raising her children as she and Dean began spending more time together.

As promised, Dean made plans later that month to spend a Saturday shooting hoops with Kayden at the home of Katie's parents.

Liam and Cody took a big liking to Dean as he spent time bonding with each of them doing activities that each child enjoyed.

Katie loved that her children were bonding with Dean. She could feel her and Dean growing closer as time went on.

Katie had decided to invite Dean over for dinner with her parents' blessing.

Dean accepted excitedly; he couldn't wait to be seated at their dinner table.

Dean loved spending time with Katie and her family.

Katie felt that the advice her mother had given her was wise, and she felt that if things were going to continue to grow between her and Dean, then this would be the next step moving forward.

Katie felt that making a stronger bond with everyone would be the best way to start moving forward, as everyone seemed to be getting along so great.

Katie wanted to keep making progress between her and Dean.

Lauren assured Katie that the connection between her and Dean was pure and that it was sure to be something bigger in the future.

As the day arrived for the family dinner with Dean, Katie sat with her children that morning at the breakfast table and talked to them about Dean coming over for dinner that evening.

The children were thrilled with the idea.

As Kayden spoke up and asked if they could shoot some hoops after dinner, Katie responded with a smile saying, "I am sure Dean would be happy to, Kayden."

Kayden replied saying "Cool!"

Later that evening, Dean arrived for dinner.

Katie greeted him at the front door and welcomed him inside.

Dean kissed Katie's cheek and told her she looked lovely.

Katie thanked him.

Her mother entered the foyer and said hello to Dean.

Dean responded to Lauren saying hello and telling her that she had a lovely home, and he thanked her for having him for dinner.

Lauren thanked Dean for his kindness.

Dean then looked at Lauren and complimented her appearance.

Lauren responded to Dean stating he was such a gentleman, as they showed him to the dining room.

As the family took their seats at the dinner table, Katie's father began conversating with Dean.

They began talking about cars bond engines.

Katie was pleased how well her father and Dean had been getting along.

Before the family began to enjoy their wonderful dinner Katie and Lauren had prepared, Katie and her family joined hands with Dean and said grace for their meal.

Everyone said amen and then began enjoying their tasty meal.

Dean complimented Katie and Lauren and said he could get used to this kind of home cooking.

As the children giggled, Katie and Lauren smiled.

After dinner, Katie cleared the table with the help of Dean and her children. Her parents retired to the family room and in their favorite chairs for the remainder of the evening.

Katie told Dean he didn't need to help clean the dinner mess, but Dean had insisted on helping.

Katie smiled and thanked Dean for his kindness.

After the kitchen was cleaned, Kayden asked Dean if he would like to shoot some hoops before he left to go home.

Dean smiled and said he would love that, especially after eating such a large meal.

Katie responded stating how great that was and that Kayden had been wanting to shoot hoops with him.

As Dean and Kayden made their way outdoors to shoot hoops, Liam and Cody followed, being their audience and hoping to take part in the game.

Katie followed her children outside and took a seat on the back porch swing her father had built for her mother.

As she watched her sons play basketball with Dean, she sat swinging with a smile on her face and her heart feeling so content.

Katie could not be happier than in that moment.

As Katie continued watching her sons play basketball with Dean, she was proud that Kayden had allowed his two younger brothers join in on the fun shooting hoops.

The sound of her children's laughter was music to her ears.

A while later after the children had spent quite some time playing basketball, Katie told them it was time to get cleaned up and ready for bed.

Dean told them he had to be getting home, too, and that he was exhausted from all the fun playing.

The children said goodbye to Dean and thanked him for playing and coming to dinner, then went inside to take their baths and get ready for bed.

As Katie told them, she would be up shortly to say good night and tuck them in.

Dean asked Katie if it were okay to say good night to her parents before leaving.

Katie responded "Of course, they would love that" as she showed him the way back in.

As Dean thanked Katie's parents once more for their hospitality and told them to have a good evening, they told Dean he was welcome to visit again soon.

Lauren spoke up and told Dean that he was a part of their family now.

Katie's father smiled and nodded with what his wife had just said.

Dean smiled and thanked them both for that, for he felt that he was truly a part of their family now.

As Katie walked Dean out to the covered front porch, he thanked her again for the lovely homecooked meal and the fun he had with her sons playing basketball.

Dean told her that she had a great family and that he could not wait to spend more time with them.

Katie smiled and told him she was happy that he felt that way because she felt she could not get him off her mind.

Dean smiled and said he had been waiting so long to hear those words.

Dean then asked if he could kiss her good night.

Katie smiled and said she would love that.

As she closed her eyes, he leaned in and pressed his soft sweet lips against hers, and the passion they both felt was a feeling of fireworks shooting off in the sky.

Katie felt her foot pop up, just as it had before with the surprise kiss Dean had done on their date at the bowling alley.

As they finished their kiss and opened their eyes, they both responded, "Wow!"

They giggled seeing that they had the same reaction to their passionate kiss.

Dean asked Katie if that was okay.

Katie responded that it was better than okay and that it was amazing.

Dean smiled and then hugged her before leaving for the evening.

As Katie watched him pull out of the driveway, she slowly made her way back inside.

Katie could not help but hear the song play in her head, "I'm in heaven, / I'm in heaven."

As her parents asked her if she was okay, Katie responded, "I am better than okay. I am great!"

As Katie made her way up the stairs to tuck her sons into bed, her parents looked at each other sitting in their favorite chairs and said, "Our Katie is in love!"

As they giggled to each other, Katie's father responded to her mother saying, "I like this one. Dean is going to be good for her and the boys."

Lauren quickly responded, stating that she should hope so, as she was the one to set them up. And then she began giggling as her husband, Phillip, made a silly face at her.

As the family grew fonder of Dean and the months turned into years, the connection between Dean and Katie grew even stronger.

Katie began to feel complete as her children asked to spend more time with Dean.

Katie felt the love and connection she had longed for since she was a teenager was finally happening to her.

Katie felt as if she knew she was living a real-life love story from one of her favorite novels. She prayed that the connection between her and Dean would continue to grow stronger and that this feeling would last forever.

As Katie's family grew happier and strongly united, Katie knew that there would come a time that Dean would want to introduce her to his side of the family.

As the time came when Katie and Dean decided to make their relationship as an official couple, they wanted to share the news with her children and her parents first.

Katie felt their reaction would set the stage for telling the news to the rest of her family and then for meeting Dean's family.

Katie sat down her sons one evening and asked them their feelings for her and Dean becoming an official couple.

Katie's children cheered with happiness and said, "Yay, finally!"

Katie's parents had been listening from the next room and came in to celebrate the news.

They had told Katie they could not be happier for her and Dean.

The next day, Katie invited Dean over to her parents' home so that she could share the news with him face to face.

Katie wanted to let Dean know that her children were excited for them to be an official couple and that her parents were too.

As Dean arrived later that afternoon and received the good news, tears of joy came to his eyes.

Dean felt he had been blessed, as he had fallen in love with Katie. He already loved her sons too, and he felt that he had been blessed with two sets of parents, being that Katie's parents had been so kind to him and welcomed him to their family.

Katie was so excited about this she really felt that things were coming together smoothly.

Katie had hoped that when she met Dean's family, they would accept her just as easily too. She hoped she would be able to bond with his family as Dean had bonded with hers and that they would be able to make their blended family a strong, happy one.

Katie's mother, Lauren, assured her that though things may take a little time with Dean's family, but everything would work out, as Dean loved her and her sons.

Lauren continued telling Katie to pray about it and for her not to worry, that worrying would just make things worse, and to give her worries to God in prayer.

Lauren continued telling her daughter to trust her and that she would see everything would be all right.

C H A P T E R   9

Meeting Dean's Family

As time went on for Katie and her sons and years passed, life had gotten better and happier for Katie and her family.

Katie felt meeting Dean was a big step for her and her children. She loved how they started out as friends and developed their friendship into a relationship over time.

Katie and Dean could not be happier as a couple, raising her three children together.

As Katie and Dean felt it was time for her to meet his family, Katie felt nervousness come over her.

Katie remembered Dean telling her in the beginning that he was close to his mother and younger brother and that he also had older sisters that were much older than him, but he wasn't very close to them.

Dean told Katie he never had a strong bond with his sisters like he had with his younger brother.

Dean assured Katie that his mother would surely welcome her and that his younger brother would be kind too.

Dean warned Katie though that his sisters may be a little harder to warm up too and that they were already set in their own ways in life.

Katie was nervous but wanted nothing more than to make Dean happy. She knew that he had gone above and beyond to get to know her family, and she wanted to do the same for him.

Dean had asked Katie if she would join him to meet his mother and younger brother one warm summer Saturday afternoon.

It was the month of July, and you could feel the sense of harmony and love in the air.

The weather outside was warm and beautiful.

Lauren, Katie's mother, had offered to watch her children to give Katie time with Dean to meet his family.

Lauren assured Katie that Dean's mother would love her and would welcome her into her home.

Katie responded to her mother that she hoped so and that she was nervous to meet her and his siblings.

Dean had made the arrangements with his mother, Rebecca, to introduce Katie to her.

Rebecca knew they had been dating for quite some time and had asked Dean if he felt this would be something to last.

Dean told his mother Rebecca that he had fallen in love with Katie and that she loved him too.

Rebecca was unsure how to feel at first, hearing her first-born son stating he was in love with Katie, for she had been in love once in her life, and that was with Dean's father.

Rebecca had married Dean's father at a youthful age and blessed him with five children: three daughters and two sons.

Though they had a happy marriage to start and years of marriage spent together raising their children, sadly their marriage fell apart, breaking Rebecca's heart forever and leaving her to raise her two young sons alone, just after her three daughters had grown and left the nest to begin their own life journeys.

After such a loss from many years married to the love of her life, Rebecca had given up on love.

And knowing that her three daughters had grown up with families of their own, she had dreaded the day that was surely to come for her sons to find love too.

Hearing her oldest son, Dean, claiming that he found true love, was disheartening for Rebecca, for though she wanted to be happy for her son, she carried the burden on her shoulders of losing her one true love.

Rebecca could not help but worry if the same would happen to her son. She wanted nothing more than to see her son happy, so she graciously extended an invitation for Dean to bring his love to meet her in her home.

Dean was overjoyed to hear his mother's invitation to meet his love, Katie. He assured his mother that in time, she would grow to love Katie as a daughter and see how she had become the love of his life.

Rebecca painted a smile for her son, though she had her own concerns with love.

Rebecca did not want her son to see her doubts where love was involved.

When the afternoon for Dean to pick up Katie from her parents' home arrived, Dean was excited. He could not wait to introduce her to his family.

Though Katie was feeling as if butterflies were in her stomach from nervousness, she wanted nothing more than to make Dean happy.

Katie had hugged her children and told them to mind their grandparents as Dean arrived in her parents' driveway.

As Dean walked up the walkway and greeted Katie and her family, Katie's parents told him it was good to see him again.

Dean responded likewise to her parents.

Katie hugged her mother and thanked her again for sitting with her children.

As her father told her make sure she had fun, Lauren responded to Katie that everything would be okay.

Lauren continued telling Katie to just be herself and that they would be sure to love her.

As Katie and Dean walked to his truck and Dean helped her inside, Katie's heart began to pound with nervousness.

Dean assured her it would be all right. He told Katie that "they were just people like you and I."

Katie could not help but worry, knowing the stories that Dean had told her—how his mother felt about love after losing the love of her life with a broken marriage.

As Katie and Dean made the hour-long trip to his mother's house, Katie could not help but sit in silence with her nervousness.

Dean squeezed her hand and told her that everything was going to be all right.

Katie nodded to say okay to Dean as the radio played soothing country music on their long drive.

As they arrived at the home of Dean's mother, Dean reminded Katie that his younger brother, Carsen, would also be home.

Dean had told Katie that Carsen would not talk much at first but, once he warmed up to her, that he had quite a unique sense of humor.

Dean continued telling Katie that his brother would make her laugh with his silly jokes once he got to know her.

Katie smiled and said, "It is good that you are close to your brother." She told Dean that it was important to have a close relationship with siblings.

Katie reminded Dean that for her growing up, her younger brother was always her best friend.

Dean smiled at Katie upon hearing this, as he remembered she had told him this before.

Dean was excited to hear that Katie was happy that he had a close relationship with his younger brother.

As they neared the long driveway to Rebecca's home, Dean had mentioned one last thing to Katie, telling her that sometimes his brother would come off as a bit rude.

Dean continued saying to Katie, "Try not to take offense to it if it happens."

Katie smiled and nodded in understanding.

As they pulled up the long dirt driveway heading up to the farmhouse of Dean's mother, Katie squeezed Dean's hand a little tighter in nervousness.

Dean smiled at her, assuring her it would be okay.

As Dean parked his truck and turned the engine off, he hopped out of his truck and opened Katie's passenger door.

As he took her hand and helped her down from the truck, he looked into her eyes and said, "Trust me. Everything will be great!"

Katie smiled as Dean led her to the long winding porch that led to Rebecca's front door.

Dean politely knocked on the door before entering, calling out for his mother to let her know they had arrived.

Rebecca was seated on her sofa in her living room with his younger brother, Carsen.

Rebecca responded to Dean saying "Come on in. We're in here."

As Dean led Katie into the kitchen, being the entryway to the living room, Katie felt her heart beating faster.

As they located Rebecca and Carsen in the living room, Dean said hello to his family as they stared in wonder looking at Katie.

Dean said, "Mom, Carsen, I would like you to meet Katie." Dean then turned to Katie and said, "Katie, I would like you to meet my mother, Rebecca, and my younger brother, Carsen."

As Rebecca said hello to Katie, Katie responded by saying "Hello, ma'am, it is very nice to meet you."

Rebecca smiled at Dean and said, "Well, you both can have a seat."

Katie and Dean seated themselves on the plaid loveseat across from Rebecca.

While Dean's younger brother, Carsen, stared in silence, Rebecca spoke up telling her son Carsen not to be rude, to say hello, and to greet their guest.

As Carsen said hello, Katie said hello once more in return.

Silence filled the room for a moment until Dean had struck up a conversation.

Dean began by asking his mother how she has been feeling and asking his brother how things have been for him.

As Rebecca spoke about her health and things going on in her life, Katie sat there patiently listening and waiting to answer any questions Rebecca may have.

As Rebecca turned the conversation to Katie and began asking her simple questions and complimenting her style. Katie thanked her and responded to her questions.

Katie told Rebecca that she hoped that her health would improve and that she had a lovely home and thanked her for inviting her.

Rebecca responded that it was not much but that she was blessed to have it.

Katie was pleased that Rebecca had been so kind and inviting to her.

As the afternoon went on, Dean and Katie continued to enjoy their visit with Dean's family.

As Dean's brother joked with Dean, Katie smiled seeing how well they got along together.

Rebecca responded to her sons, telling them to keep their jokes clean and stating that they had a lady in their presence.

Dean smiled at the thought that his mother was warming up to Katie.

As Katie sat there feeling more relaxed seeing that Dean's family was warming up to her, she felt like her angels were smiling down at her, letting her know that everything would be okay.

As the afternoon ended, Dean told his mother that he needed to get Katie back home.

Rebecca thanked them for visiting her and told Katie it was so nice to meet her, and she invited her to visit again soon.

Katie graciously thanked Rebecca for having her for a visit and told her she hoped to visit her again soon.

Rebecca smiled stating that she would love that, and she told Katie that she hoped to meet her three sons one day too.

Dean smiled at his mother and responded to her saying "All in good time, Mom, all in good time."

"Baby steps first," Dean stated to his mother.

Rebecca nodded in agreement with her son.

As Rebecca walked Dean and Katie to the front door to say their goodbyes for the day, Dean hugged his mother and told her he loved her. Rebecca smiled at her son and then turned to Katie telling her once more that it was so nice to meet her.

Carsen waved at the couple as they exited out the door and as Dean held Katie's hand and walked with her to his truck to return to the home of Katie's parents.

As Dean helped Katie into the truck and then hopped into the driver's seat, he turned and looked at Katie and said, "I love you. Thank you for doing this for me!"

Katie smiled at Dean and said, "I love you too!"

Katie continued telling Dean she enjoyed meeting his family and that she loved making him happy.

As Dean started his truck and began driving down the long driveway back to the home of Katie's parents, Dean felt as if he was flying on a cloud of happiness.

Katie, seated beside him in his pickup truck, was smiling ear to ear seeing how happy Dean was.

Katie felt as if things were going great, and she could not wait to get back home to her children and her parents and let her mother know how things went meeting Dean's family.

As Dean and Katie arrived back at the home of Katie's parents, Katie's mother was in the backyard sitting at her picnic table and watching her grandsons playing.

Katie and Dean walked over to her mother and greeted her and said hello to her children as they enjoyed the warm outdoor weather.

Katie's children came running to her as they saw she arrived back home.

Smiling, Katie said "Hi, my sons" as she greeted them with open arms.

Dean high-fived her sons as they greeted him.

Lauren smiled seeing her family so happy.

Lauren then asked her daughter how things went with the visit to Dean's mother.

Katie said, "Surprisingly, things went well."

Katie continued telling her mother that she was nervous for nothing.

Lauren smiled and responded to her saying, "See I told you, Katie, everything would be fine."

Katie thanked her mother for the encouragement and for watching her children.

Lauren stated it was her pleasure and that she loved time with her grandchildren.

Lauren continued telling Katie that it made her heart feel so full having time with her grandchildren.

Katie loved hearing these words from her mother, for she only wanted happiness for her loving mother who had done so much for everyone and never asked for anything in return.

Katie was determined to repay her mother's kindness somehow someday.

As the day was ending, Dean told Katie that he better get home and that he had some things he needed to finish to prepare for his upcoming work week.

Katie thanked Dean for the afternoon spent together and for taking her to meet his family.

Dean told her that he would like for her to meet his three oldest sisters sometime when she was available.

Katie smiled and said okay to Dean and that she would like that.

As Dean said his goodbyes to Lauren and Katie's children and kissed Katie good night, he headed back to his truck to return to his home for the evening.

Dean honked and then waved goodbye to Katie and her family as he pulled out of the driveway.

Katie told her children it was time to go in and clean up for the night and prepare for dinner.

As Katie and her children went inside with her mother, Lauren told Katie she was happy she had a good day.

Katie hugged her mother and told her she was the best as her mother kissed her on her head.

As the children cleaned up for dinner, Katie told her mother to rest and that she would prepare a quick dinner and put the children to bed.

Lauren thanked Katie for that.

Katie responded it was her pleasure and that she loved cooking and that it was her time to take care of her mother now.

It was Katie's way of trying to repay her mother for all her mother had done for her all throughout her life and to show her mother that she and her children were her everything, even with Dean being a part of their lives now.

As Katie and her family gathered at the dinner table and Katie served everyone their dinner, Lauren and the children thanked Katie for the delicious meal.

As Katie smiled and asked her son Kayden to say grace, Lauren smiled as she lowered her head for Kayden to say grace.

As the family said amen, they continued their time together having their dinner and conversation over how everyone's day went.

After dinner, Katie and her sons cleared the table and cleaned the dishes as Katie's parents retired to their bedroom for the evening.

Katie and her sons finished their cleaning duties, then she had her children prepare for bed and then headed upstairs herself to tuck her children in and take time for herself before retiring to bed for the evening.

As Katie lay in her queen-sized bed, she lay there staring out her skylights above her bed.

Katie said her prayers and then lay there in her bed with love in her heart. She was thankful for her life.

Katie was excited about what the future had in store for her and her children. She could not wait to see what the next chapter of her life held for her and her children.

Katie promised herself that no matter what, she would be the best mother to her children—always putting them first—and that she would care for her mother the best she could as she always took care of her, for Lauren, being the best mother that she was, always put her children first.

Katie also promised herself to always remain close to her father, being that growing up, she was close to her father, and her father would tell her she was daddy's little girl.

The next morning, Katie was awoken by her children jumping on her bed saying "Wake up, Mom, wake up!" laughing.

Katie sat up, smiled, and said, "This is the best way to wake up." She felt so blessed to have three beautiful sons to wake up to, knowing that her life purpose was to raise them to be good men one day.

Katie felt her heart overflow with love, and she could not wait to see what the day had held.

As Katie began her day with her children, having breakfast with her family, her parents had begun speaking to Katie about a new home that had come available to rent in the same town where Dean had lived.

It was a short trip from the house of Katie's parents, and Katie's parents felt that it would be good for her and her children to have their own place.

Lauren and Phillip told Katie that with her having Dean in their lives now, it would be a good thing for her to start this new chapter in their own home.

Katie agreed with her parents that though it was great being back home, she felt that her parents were right and that it was time to get back to having her own home again for her and her sons.

As Katie and her parents talked about the rental property, Katie's oldest son, Kayden, got excited.

Kayden said to his mother, "I think it sounds great! Let's check it out!"

Katie agreed with Kayden and said, "I will call the number after breakfast, and we will go from there."

Lauren smiled telling Katie she was making the right decision for her and her children.

CHAPTER 10

Katie's New Family Home

As Katie and her family finished breakfast, Katie's sons offered to clean up the breakfast table and dishes so that Katie could make the call for the rental property.

Katie went into her parents' home office to make the call for the rental home.

Katie's parents and sons waited eagerly to see what would come of the call.

As the owner of the property answered the phone and Katie introduced herself and explained the reason for her call, the homeowner began telling Katie everything she needed to know about the property.

Katie was extremely excited and had decided to set up an appointment with the owner for her and her sons to visit the property for a showing.

The owner had instructed Katie that he would be there later that afternoon if she would like to come then.

Katie told the homeowner of the rental property that it sounded like a plan.

As the owner continued providing Katie with the address and the time to meet him there, Katie thanked him and then hung up the phone.

As Katie opened the office door, she returned to the family room, where her parents and sons had been waiting for her. Katie told her family she had scheduled an appointment to see the rental property that afternoon.

Her sons cheered with joy, as they were excited to have a new home.

Though they loved living with their grandparents, they felt that they were getting older, and it was time to be back in their own home again.

Lauren told Katie that was great news and that she was sure that she would be happy having her own home again.

Lauren continued with telling Katie that with her having Dean in her life, it was time that she had her own space.

Lauren then explained to Katie that her father was getting older, and she was too; and with this being said, they felt that though they loved having them there, they felt this would be the best for everyone, that for Katie to be getting a new home for herself and her children.

Katie agreed with her mother, stating that she had been wanting to move to her own home for a while now.

Katie continued telling her mother that it was just that she didn't know when the timing would be best for everyone for her to do this.

Katie's father spoke up and told her that everything worked out as it should and that he had no doubt that things would work out great for her and his grandsons.

Katie hugged her father and thanked him for being the best father she could ask for.

Katie then hugged her mother and told her she would miss their morning talks and their everyday chats together.

Lauren assured Katie that even if they did not see each other every day, they would still be talking on the phone several times a day every day.

Katie hugged her mother and thanked her for being so wonderful. She told her mother she would not be the person she was today if it had not been for her motherly love.

Katie then hugged her father and thanked him for the wisdom and the discipline he gave her.

As the day continued, the time came for Katie and her sons to visit the rental property in the small town where Dean lived.

Katie could feel herself getting excited. Her children were excited about the new adventure they were about to embark on, knowing that they were going to have their own home again.

As Katie and her children loaded into their car and began their trip to the rental property, excitement filled the air.

Katie asked her children if they were excited to see the home that could possibly become their new home.

The children shouted yes.

Katie laughed and said that was all she needed to hear.

As they arrived at the rental property, the homeowner had already arrived and had been waiting for Katie and her children in the driveway.

The property owner waved at Katie and her children as they pulled into the drive.

The property was quite nice, better than the owner had described on the phone.

Katie was pleased to see such a large yard and at how lovely the home looked on the outside.

As she parked her car, she and her sons stepped out and smiled, acknowledging how nice the property looked from the outside.

Katie greeted the owner and introduced herself and her children.

As he told her it was a pleasure to meet them, he led the way for them to go inside.

As they entered the rental home, Katie was amazed at how lovely it looked.

The home had a country theme to it for the decoration and was much larger than she had expected.

The owner had told her the home had three bedrooms and one bathroom and that there was a detached garage included.

Katie smiled, as she loved how the home looked inside and out. Her children began exploring the home and calling out which room would be theirs, should their mother choose to rent it.

The owner had told Katie how much the rent would be and the security deposit.

Katie assured him that it was affordable and that she loved the property.

After accessing the property, the owner asked Katie her thoughts on it.

Katie responded with "I love it," then asked her sons what they thought. Her sons responded with "We love it! We want to live here."

The owner laughed and said, "You boys will love the school here too."

Katie smiled and said, "Well, I think we'll take it."

The owner smiled and said, "Well, I think your family will be very happy here."

As the owner made arrangements with Katie to do the paperwork on the following business day, the property owner told Katie that he was happy to have her as a tenant and that he felt she and her sons would feel right at home there.

Katie thanked him once more and then told her children to load back into the car so they could go home and tell their grandparents the great news.

As Katie and her sons arrived back at her parents' home, her sons were extremely excited.

They could not wait to tell their grandparents the great news about their new home.

As they pulled into the drive at their grandparents' home, Katie put her car into park and turned off the engine.

Katie's sons jumped out and ran up the walkway to their grandparents' front door.

Katie was pleased to see how excited her sons were over the news of getting their own home. She knew they loved being with their grandparents, but they were getting older.

Katie knew her parents were right with this being the next best step for her and her children.

As her sons reached the front boor of her parents' home, they ran inside shouting "Grandma, Grandpa, we're back!"

Katie followed behind them, stating there was no reason to shout indoors.

As her children were filled with excitement when they located their grandparents in the family room, their grandparents smiled and said, "Oh my, you boys are sure excited."

Katie's three sons began talking at the same time, stating they got a new home.

Lauren, laughing at the children's excitement, told them, "*Okay, boys, one at a time please.*"

Suddenly, Kayden spoke up and said, "Mom got us a new home."

"We are moving next weekend," Kayden stated.

Lauren clapped, as she felt this was great news for Katie and her children.

As Liam and Cody jumped up and down with excitement, Katie then proceeded to tell her parents that she had decided to rent the property and that it was even nicer than described on the phone.

Katie continued to speak how the schools were great and that the neighborhood was kid friendly.

Katie told her parents it would be a drive to work, also that it was a short commute to visit them and that it was closer to Dean.

Katie's parents told her that was great news, and they were happy for her and her children.

Katie assured her parents that she would still be there for them and help take care of their needs as well.

Lauren responded to Katie telling her that she was certain Katie would still be there for her and her father.

Lauren continued to assure Katie that her siblings would be there, too, should they need them to help.

As Katie and her family prepared for their week ahead, excitement filled her parents' home.

Katie felt as if things were getting even better for her and her children. A new chapter was about to begin for them, and she was extremely excited about this.

It had been a long time coming. Katie felt her prayers were being answered, and with the help of her parents, things were turning out beautifully.

Katie could not wait to call Dean and tell him all about her new home and all the excitement that it had brought for her and her family.

As the day ended and everyone had their needs met and Katie had tucked her children into their beds for the night, Katie had decided to give Dean a call.

Katie wanted to make sure she had told Dean about the news before the new week had begun.

As Katie dialed Dean's number and waited for him to answer, she bit her lower lip in anticipation.

Katie could barely hold the excitement in.

As Dean answered the phone saying hello, Katie replied with excitement in her voice saying hi.

Katie began telling Dean her good news.

Dean responded that was wonderful news to hear. He told her he was so happy for her and her sons.

Katie thanked him for sharing her happiness and then continued to tell him that they would be moving into their new home that coming weekend.

Dean immediately offered to help Katie and her sons move, stating that he was certain they could have it all done on Saturday before the sun went down.

Katie responded thanking him for offering his help and told him that would be great.

Katie thanked Dean once more for offering his help and then stated she better let him get some rest as their workday would be coming early morning.

As Katie said good night, Dean responded, "Good night, my sweet angel. Congratulations again on your new home."

Katie thanked him once more before hanging up the phone.

As she began to retire to her bedroom for the night, she found herself filled with excitement.

Katie felt enormously proud, for she was accomplishing a new chapter in her life. She was getting a new beginning for her and her sons.

Katie felt as if she was walking on air, feeling light as a feather floating with happiness.

As Katie entered her room, she quickly prepared herself for bed. As she climbed onto her queen-sized bed, she could not help but feel the excitement still racing through her body.

As Katie lay down her head and said her prayers, she slowly drifted off to sleep. She dreamed of her future and how lovely it was to be, but her dreams were interrupted by the screaming of her alarm clock.

Katie knew the night would be short, but it had gone faster than she had anticipated.

As Katie woke and squinted her eyes from the sun shining through the windows, she could not help but feel it would be a long workday, with the night seeming to go so short.

As Katie began her day and helped her children prepare for their day, she greeted her parents' good morning as she carried the feeling of excitement with her, knowing that, by the end of the week, she and her children would be living in their new home.

It was a bittersweet feeling knowing she was leaving the comfort of her parents' home.

As the family began their day and continued their routine, they felt as if the day had passed by them quickly.

Before they knew it, the day was over. As night fell upon them, Katie knew it was just a few more days before her and her sons would move.

Katie decided to invite Dean over for dinner, with her parents' blessing, to prepare for their big move.

Katie and her family were extremely excited for moving day, as they would be sure to create so many new cherished memories.

As Katie and Dean sat down for dinner with Katie's parents and her sons, they felt the dinner was a bittersweet moment. For moving forward, they would be having their family dinners together in their new home.

Katie and her sons knew they would miss the time spent with Katie's parents and her sons' grandparents. They promised to cherish all the memories they made in her parents' home forever.

As the family finished their dinner and prepared for their big move, Dean pulled Katie aside and told her he had a question for her.

Katie felt alarmed, concerned that something was wrong, though Dean assured her everything was great.

Dean told Katie that his sisters would like to meet her when she had a free afternoon after she was done with her move and settled in.

Katie felt the same nervousness come over her, as it had when she went to meet Dean's mother and brother.

Dean told Katie there was no need to be concerned and that his sisters would treat her kindly, and it would make him so happy to introduce her to the rest of his family.

Katie smiled and agreed to Dean's request.

Worry began to sit into the back of Katie's head, for Dean always told Katie he had never been close to his sisters, given that they were extremely hard to please.

Katie remembered the stories Dean told her, of how they left their family's home when he was still young in high school and of the anger Dean felt being abandoned by his sisters.

Katie only wanted to make Dean happy, so she continued smiling and told Dean it would be great meeting his older sisters in hopes that they would be kinder in person once they got to know her and meet her children one day.

Katie loved Dean with her whole heart, as he loved her with all his, and he loved her children as his own.

The thought of Dean going through unhappiness at the hands of his family growing up just broke Katie's heart.

Katie swore she would protect her true love and not allow anyone to hurt him ever again.

As the evening grew late, Katie told her children to say good night to Dean, and then she said goodnight to Dean herself as she walked him out so that he could return home.

Dean promised Katie that he would return early so that they could spend Saturday morning moving.

Dean kissed Katie good night and told her "Sleep well, my sweet angel" as he walked away to his truck.

Katie waved goodbye to Dean and returned inside to attend to her children.

As Katie helped tuck her children into bed and then prepared to retire for the night herself, she could not get the thought out of meeting Dean's sisters out of her head.

For Dean had told her too many stories about his childhood and how his sisters could be kind when they chose to and the oldest one being the evilest of them all.

Katie was optimistic that when she met them, that they would see how much she loved Dean and how much Dean loved her and her children.

Katie hoped they would welcome her with open arms, just as Dean's mother and brother had.

As Katie lay down her head on her pillow, she fell asleep quickly. For the busy days and raising her family had taken her strength.

Katie knew she had to get plenty of rest for her journey ahead with her move for her family.

As night turned into day, Katie awakened with the screaming of the alarm clock.

Katie woke up her children and greeted them good morning. She told her children, "We have a busy day ahead of us, so let's have a good breakfast."

As they began their morning, Dean arrived early with coffee for Katie and her parents. He was smiling, and Katie thanked him as he told her he would go ahead and begin loading the moving truck.

Lauren smiled at Katie and said, "You have a good one there, daughter."

Katie smiled back at her mother and said, "It is all thanks to you for introducing us."

As Katie and her family quickly finished their breakfast and hurried to prepare for the day, they met up with Dean outside and began helping him load the moving truck.

Katie smiled as she continued loading the truck. She felt a sense of pride knowing that her demanding work and dedication to her family was the reason she had gotten this far in her life.

Katie felt grateful to everyone that had helped her along her path, and she felt very blessed to have such a wonderful family and a good man in her life.

As Katie and Dean finished loading the moving truck, Katie and her children hugged her parents and thanked them again for their love and support and for allowing them to stay there with them.

Lauren began to cry tears of sorrow, knowing that her days would be forever changed with Katie and her sons moving on.

Phillip hugged his wife and assured her they would be okay just the two of them in their home together.

Katie assured her mother that she would not be far away and that if she needed her for anything, any reason, she was a phone call away.

Lauren assured Katie that she and her father would be fine, then hugged her daughter and grandsons and told them she loved them.

Katie told her mother she loved her, too, and thanked her one more time.

Katie continued to hug her father and thanked him for everything too.

Katie then told her sons to hug their grandparents before saying goodbye.

Dean shook the hand of Katie's father and then hugged her mother.

Dean then thanked them one more time for their hospitality and for introducing him to their daughter.

Katie's parents smiled and told them to drive safely and to call them when they made it to their new home.

Katie promised her parents she would as she helped her children get into her car and then climbed into the driver seat.

Katie's parents watched them pull out of their driveway and drive away as they waved goodbye with tears in their eyes.

As Katie and Dean arrived at her new home with her children, excitement filled the car.

Katie told her sons they had arrived, and the children cheered.

Katie took a moment and called her parents as promised and told them they had made it to their new home safely and assured them she would call again soon.

As Katie and Dean began unloading the moving truck, her sons helped with excitement.

Katie thanked Dean once more as they finished unloading.

As they emptied the truck, Katie told everyone she would order pizza delivery for their first night at their new home, and her children began jumping up and down, stating this was their best day ever.

As the pizza delivery arrived, Katie called out for her sons, stating pizza was there.

As she enjoyed their first night's supper in her new home with her sons and Dean, Katie smiled seeing how happy her family was. She felt it was an amazing feeling having her very own home again.

Katie told her children that once everyone was finished with their meal, they all would have to work together and prepare their bedrooms for their bedtimes. Her sons nodded in acknowledgment as they finished their pizza, as they were excited to be sleeping their first night in their brand-new bedrooms.

Katie smiled at her children, knowing everything she had done in her life was for them.

CHAPTER 11

Meeting Dean's Sisters

As Katie and her sons settled into their new home happily, Katie kept her promise to her parents and visited often.

Katie and Dean had grown even closer and felt more in love than ever.

Katie knew that the time had come to honor her promise to Dean and meet his older sisters. Though she was nervous, Katie wanted to see her love happy.

When the day came for Dean to ask her to join him once more at his family's farm to meet his older sisters, Katie accepted with a smile.

Katie had not known how his sisters would welcome her or how they would feel about her and Dean's relationship.

Dean had told Katie that his sisters had bitterness toward the thought of him being in love with a woman that already had children, but for Dean, he loved Katie's sons as if they were his own.

Dean, being the loving, gentle man that he was, only wanted to show Katie and her sons true happiness in life, as the world had its own way of showing its ugly shadows at times.

Dean had confirmed with his family to bring Katie the following weekend for an introduction.

Katie had set things up with her parents for her sons to spend a few hours with their grandparents.

Everything was going to work out happily, Katie felt.

With the assurance from Dean and her parents, Katie felt Dean's sisters would welcome her into the family, just as Rebecca and Carsen did.

What the future held though, neither Dean nor Katie would have seen coming.

For what Dean's sisters had in mind for Dean's future did not include Dean having his own life with a wife and children.

Neither Dean nor Katie would have been prepared for what the sisters had planned for them.

As Katie and her sons settled into their new home and her sons began their new school, making new friends and staying in touch with their old friends, Katie stayed working hard with her career in the medical field all while balancing her duties as a loving mother caring for her children and spending quality time with them and while keeping up with her lovely new home.

Katie was sure to keep her promise to her parents and attended to their needs while being the best daughter to them she could be.

Katie and Dean made sure to spend as much time together as they could. For they both had busy work schedules and family demands, they both were understanding of each other's needs and made the best of both worlds.

Katie and Dean felt that their love could carry them through anything. They were determined to make their love last forever.

As Katie and her family went through their week living their daily lives, she made sure that she had plenty of time with Dean.

For the love she carried for Dean could light the world, she felt. When Dean whispered the words to her "I love *you*," Katie felt as if her heart would burst with happiness.

As for Dean, he felt the same, for he anticipated a text message from her, and he could not get her off his mind.

Katie was Dean's sunrise and sunset. He felt he waited his whole life for her and that the universe finally granted his wish of finding true love, giving him his own family that he had longed for his whole life.

Though Dean was not blessed with children of his own, he felt that Katie's children were a blessing to him, as he loved her children as if they were his own.

Dean bonded quickly with Katie's children, and for him, that meant everything.

Dean anticipated the day he would get down on one knee and ask Katie to marry him after getting her parents' permission first.

Dean wanted nothing more than to make their family complete.

Katie and Dean had been a couple for an exceptionally long time now. The love he felt for Katie and her sons, Dean did not want another day to pass by without making Katie his wife and having her officially take his last name.

Dean wanted nothing more than to give Katie and her sons the family they deserved: a husband and father figure, which Katie and her sons longed for.

As the weekend arrived for Katie to meet Dean's sisters, Katie felt the nervous butterflies in her stomach.

Though her mother Lauren and Dean assured her that his sisters would love her, Katie felt her intuition was warning her that danger lurked with them.

Katie continued feeling that they would not accept her. She decided to smile through it though, as she wanted nothing more than to make Dean happy.

As the time neared for Katie and Dean to leave for his mother's home, they dropped Katie's sons off with her parents and assured them they would be back by supper.

Katie hugged her sons and told them she loved them, and she hugged her mother and thanked her once more.

Dean high-fived Katie's sons and promised to be back by supper, and he hugged Lauren and thanked her again for everything she had done.

Lauren told Katie and Dean she loved them both and to drive safely.

As Katie and Dean stepped out the door of her parents' home and made their way to Dean's truck, Lauren stepped out onto the porch and shouted out to Katie and Dean wishing them good luck with the sisters while smiling, hoping to help relieve the tension Katie was feeling.

Katie and Dean smiled and waved goodbye to Lauren as she and Dean left the drive.

As Katie and Dean began the journey to his mother's home, Dean assured Katie that everything would be fine.

Dean told Katie, "My sisters can be a bit much, but I am certain they want to see me happy."

Katie smiled and nodded, silently thinking that she hoped so.

As they neared the home of Dean's mother, Dean began to speak, telling Katie more about his sisters. He told Katie, "You know my oldest sister is Layla. She can be a bit much."

Dean continued telling Katie that "Layla was always my father's favorite and my mother's too."

Dean continued telling Katie that his mother would only say that if you angered her as a teenager or had a disagreement with her as an adult, he joked.

Katie smiled back at Dean as she continued to listen.

Dean continued telling Katie that Layla was a bit of a controlling person and that she was used to having her way.

Dean told Katie not to be alarmed though, that Layla never approved of anything, and that their family just looked past it.

Dean continued describing Layla as a person that loved controlling everything and everyone and that his family gave Layla the nickname Control Freak!

Katie gasped in reaction to the nickname for Layla as Dean smiled and told Katie that she would see this about Layla in time.

Dean then began speaking about his middle sister Journey. He talked about how she had helped his mother with him when he was just an infant and that he felt in a way that she was his guardian angel, always looking out for him.

Dean spoke about how after she had grown up and married and begun her own family, they had grown apart but that she always held a special place in his heart.

Dean continued to tell Katie that Journey was a sensitive soul and "You had to be careful with your words, for she gets upset easily, and you had to be gently speaking with her."

Katie smiled and said she understood, for she, too, had a sister that was the same way.

Dean told Katie he felt that Journey would want him to be happy and that she would welcome Katie with open arms.

Dean became silent in his thoughts for a moment, for he feared Journey would be eager to please her sisters and mother; and if they had not approved of Katie, she would not either.

Dean tried to hide his silent fears from Katie, as he did not want to upset her or make her more nervous than she already was feeling.

Dean continued to speak about his youngest sister Skylar, whom he described as "always seeking attention."

Dean talked about how she would do anything to please their mother and how she always needed help with anything life threw at her.

Dean continued telling Katie that Skylar could be the sweetest person you knew, as long as you stayed on her sweet side, and that if you angered her and got on her bad side, she would be quick to turn on you.

Katie felt concerned with this, for she wondered how Dean could be so sweet and have sisters like villains.

Dean hoped that by being opened to Katie about his sisters that this would help her understand them better.

Dean began thinking about all he had done to help his sister Skylar over the many years they grew up together. He hoped that Skylar would repay him for his kindness by showing kindness to his love, Katie, and helping him with their sisters Layla and Journey to warm up to Katie.

Dean would later learn that Skylar, too, would be evil and team up with Layla to try and destroy his relationship with Katie and their family.

Dean reached out for Katie's hand. She took his hand in hers and squeezed it. Katie gave him a smile assuring him everything would be okay.

As they arrived at the home of Dean's mother, Dean saw his sisters had already arrived. He felt a lump in his throat as he tried to swallow. Nervousness came over Dean, but he tried to hide it from Katie.

Katie squeezed Dean's hand, as she saw him tensing up. She asked him if he was okay.

As Dean responded yes and then let a dry cough, Dean apologized to Katie, stating it had been many years since he introduced anyone to his sisters.

Katie assured him that it was okay and that she was ready for the introduction.

Dean turned to Katie stating that he loved her and that she was the best thing that had happened to him.

Katie responded by telling Dean she loved him, too, and that he completed her.

As Dean turned off the engine and jumped down from his truck, making his way to the passenger door to help Katie down, Katie thanked him for his politeness and help, as Dean lifted her flirtingly down from the truck.

Katie smiled in happiness as they stood hand in hand.

Dean looked at her and said, "Shall we do this?"

Katie nodded stating yes.

As they made their way up the long winding porch to the front door of Rebecca's home, Dean prepared to knock as the front door flew open.

It had been Skylar, Dean's youngest sister, standing there eagerly waiting to greet them and welcome them inside.

Dean smiled as Skylar hugged him and said, "Good to see you, little brother."

Dean laughed in excitement and told her it was good to see her too.

Skylar invited Dean and Katie inside, stating that everyone was waiting for their arrival.

Katie felt her heart racing with nervousness. She was not sure what to expect with Dean's family being all together.

Katie smiled as Dean led her inside his mother's home.

As Katie followed Dean into his mother's kitchen, his family had been sitting around the dining table conversating and smiling.

As Rebecca greeted her son saying hello and greeting Katie telling her it was lovely to see her again, Katie responded to Rebecca saying it was lovely to see her again too.

As Dean's older sisters stared in curiosity, Dean turned to Katie and began introducing her to his sisters one by one.

As his first introduction began with his oldest sister Layla, Layla responded to Katie saying hello as she chomped on her chewing gum, giving Katie a death stare.

Katie responded politely saying hello and that it was lovely to meet her.

Then Dean turned to his second sister, Journey, and began introducing her to Katie.

As Journey responded to Katie that it was nice to meet her, Katie responded that it was her pleasure to meet her as well.

As Dean turned to Skylar, she had been smiling stating that Dean saved the best for last.

Dean laughed and jokingly stated "yes, for sure."

Dean stated, "Skylar, I would like you to meet the love of my life, Katie."

As Skylar responded "Wow, you are pretty," Katie blushed saying thank you and responded that she was too.

As everyone began to settle in for their visit, Dean's brother, Carsen, entered the room as everyone looked and said hello.

Carsen laughed and jokingly asked, "Is this a party for me?"

As everyone began laughing with him, the energy in the air seemed to calm, and Katie and Dean started to feel more relaxed.

Rebecca remained seated in her favorite chair as the family took their seats around her.

Everyone began talking about how life had been for everyone and sharing memories.

Katie felt as if things were going to be great.

Dean's family had welcomed her with open arms, and laughter filled the air.

Dean was smiling from ear to ear, and for Katie, that was all the confirmation she needed that the family was accepting of her.

As Katie spoke with Dean's sisters one on one and learned more about them, she felt as if she gained new sisters.

Katie began letting her walls down and felt that Dean's sisters would be safe to let in. Katie felt as if there was so much love in the air.

As the day continued and dinner time was nearing, Dean told his mother and his siblings that they had to be getting back to the children.

Dean told his mother that they promised the children they would be back by supper to pick them up from their grandparents' home.

Rebecca hugged her son and told Katie it was nice seeing her again and to visit again soon.

Katie responded it was a pleasure as always to see her, and she turned to Dean's siblings telling them it was so nice to meet them too.

Dean told everyone goodbye, and Katie said goodbye to everyone once more and thanked them again for having her.

Dean led Katie to the door, then walked with her hand in hand down the porch and helped her up into his truck.

Katie thanked Dean for his assistance with helping her into the truck and told him she had a wonderful time.

Dean smiled as he climbed into the driver's seat, stating that he thought the overall visit had gone well. He told Katie that he felt that his sisters liked her and that things would be great moving forward.

Katie smiled and assured Dean that she felt the same.

Katie couldn't shake the feeling that Layla despised the fact that Dean was with her and that Dean brought her to his mother's to meet his sisters, whereas Journey and Skylar were so polite, conversating with Katie as if they've known her forever.

Katie couldn't help but wonder if his sisters were truly welcoming her. Or was it all a play to make their brother Dean happy?

Katie felt that her heart had been hitting her head. Given the love she had for Dean, she longed for his family to accept her and welcome her and her children.

But knowing what Dean had shared with her about how his sisters could be villains alarmed Katie.

Katie felt she had to maintain walls around her heart when it came to Dean's sisters, though she truly wanted to take them down.

Katie knew she had to protect her heart from false people moving forward. Though she was willing to give Dean's sisters a chance, Katie wasn't going to allow his sisters to destroy her emotionally, should they be wearing false masks with their kindness.

As Dean drove down the long driveway leaving his mother's home, Katie felt a cold chill down her spine, as if someone was watching them leave from behind.

As she turned to look, Katie noticed Layla standing on her mother's porch with a cold, dark stare in her eyes.

Layla watched as Dean and Katie left the driveway and proceeded back to the home of Katie's parents.

Katie felt Layla's stare reminded her of something from a scary horror movie.

Katie felt alarmed, as she was no stranger to a person acting cold the way Layla had been acting. Katie knew this meant a sign of trouble with Layla, and she was determined to not let Layla wreck the happiness that she and Dean had found with each other and her sons.

Katie remembered how Dean had told her before that Layla was very controlling and that she could be very evil in her ways. Though Katie felt that she and Dean were brought together by fate, she wasn't going to allow Layla's coldness to determine her and Dean's future.

As Katie enjoyed the ride back to her parents' home with Dean, she smiled knowing that she was with the love of her life.

Katie felt a calm come over her when Dean turned and smiled at her and told her he loved her.

Katie whispered back to Dean, "I love you too, more than you know."

Dean squeezed Katie's hand as her heart fluttered with happiness, allowing Katie to forget about the coldness she felt from Layla and to focus on the moment she was in with Dean.

The Proposal

As Dean and Katie arrived back at the home of Katie's parents, Katie's children greeted them from the front porch of their grandparents' home.

Katie and Dean smiled and waved as they made their way up the walkway to the front porch.

Katie hugged her children and told them how she missed them.

Dean high-fived the children as Lauren invited everyone to come inside.

As everyone gathered in the family room, Lauren insisted they all stay for dinner.

She made her famous pot roast with all the fixings.

Katie smiled and thanked her mother for the invitation. She accepted gracefully, for she always appreciated her mother.

As Katie and the children assisted Lauren in the kitchen, Dean visited Katie's father in the family room.

Katie's father enjoyed the time he spent with Dean.

Katie's father considered Dean family, with Dean and Katie being so close.

As Dean began speaking to Katie's father, he said, "Sir, I need to ask you a question, if I may."

Katie's father looked at Dean and said, "What is on your mind tonight, son?"

Dean said, "Well, sir, I would like to ask your permission to marry your daughter."

Dean continued speaking to Phillip, stating he loved his daughter and his grandsons with all his heart and that he would like to be the husband Katie deserved and the father figure his grandsons needed.

Dean continued speaking how much he loved them all.

Dean spoke about how he loved the children as his own and how he always wanted children but life got away from him and never had the opportunity to have his own.

Katie's father looked up at Dean and said, "Son, I know my daughter loves you too. You have my blessing to take her hand in marriage. Welcome to the family, son, officially."

Dean shook Phillip's hand and thanked him.

Dean assured him that he would need Lauren's and the children's blessings also before he could officially propose to Katie.

Phillip assured Dean that he would receive their blessings as well.

Phillip told Dean, "You're family, son, and I have no doubt everyone will be excited as I am for you and Katie to marry."

Dean thanked him once more for his words of wisdom and took a breath of relief, knowing that he had received the blessing of Katie's father.

Suddenly, Katie walked into the room and told her father and Dean that dinner was ready.

As they walked with Katie to the dining room, Lauren and the children were seated at the table waiting for everyone.

Smiles and happiness filled the air as everyone took their seats, and Lauren began saying the family prayer, expressing her thanks to God for all the many blessings her family had received.

Everyone said amen.

The family continued to begin enjoying their supper.

Sounds of delight filled the room as everyone complimented Lauren on such a delicious meal.

Katie began speaking, telling her mother that she was the best cook ever.

Lauren smiled and said, "Thank you, sweetheart."

As Katie's father spoke up and told Dean that he was a lucky man, for Katie learned how to cook from her mother, Dean smiled and assured him that he was a blessed man.

Her father shook his head yes in agreement.

Once dinner was finished, Dean and the children cleared the table and helped with the dishes, while Katie took a few moments to visit her elderly father.

Once Dean was done helping the children with the kitchen chores, he took some time to speak with Katie's mother.

As Dean began to speak with Lauren, he explained how much he loved her daughter and grandsons.

Lauren replied, telling Dean she knew he loved them a lot.

Lauren continued asking Dean if everything was okay.

Dean replied with "Yes, ma'am, everything is great! I am a very blessed man."

Dean continued speaking, telling Lauren the reason he wanted to speak to her was that he wanted to ask her blessing to marry her daughter.

Tears of joy rolled down Lauren's cheek as she said "Of course, Dean, you have my blessing!"

Lauren continued telling Dean she was so proud of him.

Lauren continued telling Dean that she could tell from the very beginning when she first met Dean at the diner as her customer that he was a good man.

Dean's eyes teared up as he thanked Lauren for her kind words.

As Dean and Lauren continued their conversation, Lauren continued telling Dean that she was thankful for him and how he was so good to her daughter and grandsons.

Lauren continued with telling Dean that she wouldn't had set her daughter up on a date with just anyone and that she felt Dean was special and was made for her daughter and grandsons.

Lauren then welcomed Dean to the family, stating she was thankful to have him as her son-in-law as she hugged Dean with tears rolling down her cheek.

Lauren asked Dean if she could give him some words of wisdom.

Dean replied, "Yes, ma'am."

As Lauren continued sharing secrets of a long, happy marriage, Lauren said, "You see, Dean, Katie's father and I have been married for many years."

Lauren explained how they lived through the Great Depression and the war.

Lauren continued explaining how her and her husband had raised eight children and had many grandchildren and great-grandchildren.

Lauren continued telling Dean that "Marriage is hard, but compromise and keep God in your marriage and always resolve your disagreements before you go to bed at night. Keep love in your heart, and always remain faithful to each other. Most importantly, remember why you fell in love with each other to begin with. Doing these things will help you have a long, happy, loving marriage."

Dean thanked Lauren for her words of wisdom. He assured Lauren that he would take her words to heart. Dean promised Lauren that he would instill her words of wisdom into his marriage to Katie.

Lauren smiled at Dean, as she knew that Dean's words would prove to be true, then she hugged Dean one more time as Katie and the children entered the room.

Katie noticed the tears her mother was wiping from her cheek and how Dean was wiping a tear away from his eye.

Katie asked her mother and Dean if everything was okay.

Her mother responded, "Yes, dear, everything is great. I'm just sharing a happy moment with Dean."

As Dean smiled and assured Katie that everything was great and that he and her mother were just sharing a happy moment. Katie smiled and said, "Well, okay then, but it's getting late, and we need to be getting the children home and to bed."

Everyone shared hugs and said their goodbyes.

Katie and Dean drove back to Katie's home.

As Katie and Dean arrived back at her new home with her children, Dean thanked Katie once more for the exciting evening and then told her and the children good night.

Dean then walked out the door to return to his home, assuring Katie and her children he would be back the next day.

As the night continued, Katie and her sons prepared for bed, settling in for the night. Katie felt she had been blessed. She could not ask for more, for she had everything she ever wanted.

Katie was blessed to be a mother and to find her true love all in one lifetime.

As the night continued and turned into morning, time seemed to pass the family by.

Dean visited Katie and her sons every day, as they were inseparable.

As the new week went on, Dean was eager for the weekend, as he planned to ask Katie's children for their blessings and propose to Katie.

Katie and Dean focused on their career and their families throughout the week. Before they knew it, the weekend arrived once more.

Dean took the opportunity to talk to Katie's sons as they played a game of basketball.

Dean told the children how much he loved their mother and them.

Dean continued with asking the children if they would give him their blessings and that he would like to marry their mother.

The children shouted out yes as they high-fived one another.

Dean continued to tell them that it meant the world to him, them giving him their blessings.

Dean promised the children that he would be the best stepfather they could ever ask for.

The children spoke up and said to him, "Dean, you already are!" They huddled together in a group hug.

Dean's eyes filled with tears as he thanked God for the blessings he had given him.

Dean continued telling the boys of his plan of how he would ask their mother to marry him.

Dean wanted it to be very romantic, as he felt Katie deserved the absolute best.

Dean began telling the children that when nighttime rolled around and the stars were out at night, he would build a small campfire in the fire ring in their backyard.

Dean continued explaining to the children that their mother was planning on doing movie night for the children in the living room later that evening, and while she was setting up movie night, he was going to be in the backyard setting it up for a romantic proposal.

Dean continued telling the children that they could help him set up the backyard for his proposal to their mother if they like.

The children quickly responded yes and that it would be awesome.

Kayden, being the oldest son, assured Dean that their mother would love that.

Kayden continued telling Dean that once he was ready to do the proposal, he would keep his younger brothers entertained with the movie.

Dean thanked Kayden for his help to make this a night to remember for Katie.

Kayden continued telling Dean, this way, they could have a little romantic alone time.

Dean patted Kayden on the back and said, "Thanks, buddy, that will help."

Liam and Cody spoke up, explaining how they wanted to help too.

Dean assured them they could all help as he high-fived them.

As the day continued and nighttime came, Katie was excited to see how her children and Dean were bonding so strongly.

Katie felt warmness in her heart knowing that Dean loved her children as his own and how he treated them as if they had been his own.

As the children began the movie, Dean noticed that Katie had begun watching it too. He took the opportunity to slip out of the room and to the backyard.

Dean quickly gathered the firewood and began the campfire.

The sky was filled with stars, and the air was warm. *What a perfect night*, Dean thought as he finished the final touches in the backyard for the perfect proposal for Katie.

Dean had sat it all up perfectly. Then he stepped back indoors and asked Katie to join him in the backyard.

Dean gave the children a thumbs up so that they could witness the proposal and be a part of the special moment.

As Dean lead Katie to the backyard, the campfire crackled romantically, the stars were shining brightly, and the air felt heavenly.

Katie turned and looked at Dean and said "What is all this?" in surprise with a smile on her face.

As Dean asked her to join him on the bench swing he had placed near the campfire, he assured her that the children were safe inside and that they were happy for them to have a little alone time.

Katie smiled and said *okay* as she turned and saw her sons smiling, staring at her and Dean through the patio window.

As Dean asked Katie to take a seat on the bench swing, he took a seat next to her and then laid a blanket across her lap.

Dean then rested his arm around her shoulders and then began pointing out the stars to her, showing Katie the big dipper and pointing out a shooting star.

Dean told Katie to make a wish, as it would be good luck.

Katie smiled and closed her eyes as she made a wish on the shooting star.

Katie couldn't help but feel that her wish was going to come true unexpectedly, as she felt so much love.

As she opened her eyes, Katie found Dean down on one knee in front of her. Dean held open a ring box with a beautiful diamond ring inside it.

Katie gasped in surprise as she said "Oh my," looking at Dean with tears of joy in her eyes.

Dean began stating how much he loved her and her children and continued stating that he had asked her children and her parents for their blessing to marry her.

Dean continued stating that they gave him their blessings.

Dean continued saying, "With that, Katie, will you do me the honor of becoming my wife and making me the happiest man on earth?"

A pulse of silence filled the air for a moment as Katie tried to catch her breath to answer Dean with tears of happiness rolling down her cheek.

Dean continued saying to Katie that he knew from the first moment he met her that it was love at first sight and that he couldn't imagine living another day without her as his wife.

As tears of happiness filled Dean's eyes, Katie said, "Yes, yes, I'll marry you. I love you so much!"

Dean slipped the ring on Katie's finger and kissed her passionately, then told her he loved her so much and that she had made him the happiest man alive.

They hugged and then quickly went inside to share the news with the children as they watched the proposal by the patio door.

The love Dean and Katie had for each other, you could feel in the air. The romance and everything had turned out so perfectly.

As Katie and Dean shared the news with the children that they were getting married, the children reacted in excitement as they gave their mother and Dean a group hug.

The children were so happy; they hoped their mother would say yes. They huddled together in a group hug and said, "Finally, Dean is officially part of our family."

Katie then told her children to go grab their jackets so that they could all go outside and enjoy the campfire Dean made and roast marshmallows and celebrate the engagement.

The children hurried and did as they were told.

As the children joined their mother and Dean by the campfire, Katie felt her heart bursting with joy as she watched Dean with the children preparing marshmallows to be roasted over the campfire.

Her sons laughter were sweet happiness, and those were music to Katie's ears.

Katie could not wait for morning to come so that she could share the news of the engagement with her parents and everyone she knew.

Katie felt as all her dreams were coming true, and her wish on the shooting start just moments before had come true.

For Katie had wished that she and Dean would be married, for he was the love of her life.

Katie felt she was living proof that dreams do come true.

Announcing the Engagement

When the next morning arrived, Katie had woken up early, as she could not wait to call her parents.

As Katie made her morning coffee, her sons were still asleep from the late-night excitement. Katie quietly made her way to her patio door and slowly opened it, being careful not to wake her children.

As she made her way outside to her patio swing, Katie sat her coffee cup down beside her on her bench. She then picked up her cell phone to dial her parents' number.

But before she could dial her parents' number, she noticed a text message from Dean.

Dean had texted her "Good morning, my sweet angel. I hope you slept well, my beautiful fiancée.

Dean continued with telling Katie that he loved her and the children. He ended the text message, telling Katie he would be by that afternoon and that he hoped she would have a wonderful day.

Katie could feel the love Dean had for her and her children. She placed her hand on her heart, and with tears in her eyes, she looked up to heaven and thanked God for an answered prayer.

Katie then began dialing her parents' number. Her parents were early risers, so she was certain they would be awake.

Katie could not wait to share the news with them about her and Dean's engagement.

As Katie's mother answered the phone, Katie greeted her mother by saying "Good morning, my loving mother."

Her mother responded with "Well, good morning my beautiful daughter. Someone woke up in a great mood!"

Katie continued stating she could not be happier this morning and that the night before had been the best night ever and that she would cherish it forever.

As Lauren began having excitement in her tone, she said, "*Okay*, you want to tell me about it?"

Katie giggled and then said, "I am getting married. Dean proposed last night. He got down on one knee under the stars. It was perfect!"

Lauren began stating how wonderful that was and then telling Katie how happy she was for her and Dean and the children. She then hurried Katie's father to the phone for him to hear the news.

As Katie shared the news with her father, her father said, "I am so happy for you, my daughter. You deserve to be happy, and Dean is a good man!"

Katie thanked her father and told him she loved him.

As her father responded telling her he loved her, too, he then handed the phone back to Lauren.

Lauren expressed that she knew Dean would be the perfect fit for Katie and her sons, and she could not be happier.

Lauren stated how she could not wait to share the news with all of Katie's siblings and the rest of their family and friends.

Lauren continued telling Katie how Dean had asked for her and her father's blessing to marry her, and they both said yes. She also said that he had asked her children as well and that her children said yes to giving their blessing.

Katie could feel tears of happiness rolling down her cheek.

Katie thanked her mother again for everything and told her she could not be happier and that she felt everything she had ever wanted since she was a child was finally coming true for her.

Lauren assured her that with hard work and faith, anything was possible.

Lauren continued telling Katie that she and Dean were going to have a blessed marriage and would be great parents together.

Lauren acknowledged that she and Katie's father had seen Katie and Dean together with the children, and she believed that everything would work out perfectly.

Katie thanked her mother again for everything she had done for her, her whole life.

Lauren responded telling Katie that it's what good loving parents do for their children: they raise them healthy, teach them wisdom, and help them to fly the nest and live life on their own.

Lauren continued telling Katie that her children would be grown one day, and they, too, would fly the nest and be living on their own. They would look back on their childhood and thank her for all she had done for them, and they would thank Dean for stepping up and being the father figure they needed.

Katie thanked her mother for her kind words and told her she loved her and her father before hanging up the phone.

Her mother told her she loved her more than words and that she was so proud of her for the mother she had become.

As Katie sat quietly on the swing for a moment, she thanked God for all her blessings and, most importantly, for her family and for bringing Dean into her life.

Katie felt Dean had been an answered prayer sent to her.

Katie then continued back inside to prepare breakfast for her children and to begin their day.

As Katie attended to her children waking up from a good night's sleep, she noticed Dean had arrived. Katie smiled as she let him inside.

Katie greeted him good morning and told him he was just in time for breakfast.

Dean smiled and said, "My favorite meal of the day."

As everyone gathered around the breakfast table and said grace and then began enjoying their hot breakfast Katie had prepared, Dean began asking Katie how she felt about joining him with the children on a visit to his mother's farm.

Dean wanted to share the news about their engagement with his family.

Katie smiled and assured him she would like that.

The children began getting excited as Dean explained they could play at the farm.

Everyone felt happy about the visit, and Dean felt it would be great, knowing that his four siblings would be at the farm with his mother.

Dean felt what better way to make the announcement that he and Katie were getting married.

Though little did Dean and Katie know that Dean's oldest sister, Layla, had already began her plans of getting Katie out of Dean's life.

The worry that Katie had felt from Layla when first meeting her was becoming a reality for the happy couple.

For the deceit Layla was planning had begun.

Layla felt the best way to do this was to turn their family against Katie.

For Layla did not approve of Katie, for she felt Katie was replacing her in the family, being that Katie would eventually become the new daughter-in-law.

Layla had been scheming, telling their mother, Rebecca, horrible things behind Dean's back.

Though Layla had only met Katie once, Layla decided that she didn't want another woman in the family.

Layla knew the only way to get Katie gone was to start a family feud with her mother and get her mother to not approve of Katie, stating that Katie would surely take Dean away from her and his siblings and that she would change their family values, given that Katie came from a loving Christian family and having set long-term goals of moving on in life.

Katie had assured Rebecca during visiting her multiple times at her home with Dean that she loved that Dean was close to his family, especially her and his brother, and that she would never try to change him and that she only wanted to share her life with him.

Layla had a way of speaking to her mother and getting her way in the end, given that Layla was very controlling.

Katie even shared her long-term goals of purchasing her very own farm one day with Rebecca.

Katie wanted to stay close to her parents to care for them.

Rebecca had assured Katie that those were wonderful plans. Rebecca could tell that Katie and Dean were very in love.

Rebecca loved how Katie and Dean's love was so special, how they treated each other with kindness, and how they both had so much faith in each other.

Rebecca told Katie this was the first time she had seen her son Dean this happy.

Rebecca felt such joy, knowing her firstborn found such happiness in his life.

When Dean and Katie arrived at Rebecca's farm with the children, Dean's siblings had already arrived and were waiting with his mother.

Rebecca had informed them that Dean had been wanting to make an announcement.

Therefore, everyone was eagerly waiting to find out what it would be.

As Dean and Katie made their way to the front door of his mother's home, Dean and Katie allowed the children to play outdoors.

Katie instructed them to play safely and stay in sight where she could check on them.

As the children began playing a game of football, Dean and Katie went indoors.

Katie could feel everyone's eyes on her as she and Dean made their way to the living room.

Katie noticed Layla giving her a hard, cold stare, which sent shivers down Katie's spine.

Katie could feel the negative energy Layla was putting off the closer she and Dean got to the living room of his mother's home to join his family.

As the rest of Dean's siblings smiled and greeted them, Rebecca patiently stayed seated on her sofa as she told Dean and Katie to have a seat.

Suddenly Skylar spoke up and said, "Well, what's the big announcement?"

As Layla began to chomp on her chewing gum loudly in anger, Dean smiled and looked at everyone and said, "Well, we're getting married!"

Suddenly, Layla let out a gasp of air and said, "You got to be kidding me." Then she turned to her mother and said, "You know that Katie is only after your farm."

Katie shocked at Layla's outburst and accusing her of such falseness, suddenly spoke up and looked at Layla and said, "I love your brother with my whole heart. How can you make these accusations about me?"

Katie then turned to Rebecca and said, "I promise you, I do not want your farm. I am planning to buy my own farm close to my parents' here very soon."

As Rebecca looked at Dean and asked him about his plans, Dean assured his mother that what Katie had said was true.

Dean continued telling his mother that Katie's parents were elderly and needed extra help and that Katie was only waiting for her dream property to be on the market and that her lease would be up in time for them to purchase their new farm.

Dean continued telling his mother that this was a lifelong dream for Katie since her youth and that her mother shared this with him as well.

As Rebecca nodded in understanding Katie's plan, she looked at Layla and said, "There, you see, there is nothing to be alarmed about."

Rebecca continued to congratulate her son and Katie on their engagement and welcomed Katie and her children to the family.

Dean's sisters, Skylar and Journey, congratulated them as well.

Carsen congratulated them and said now he had someone else to joke with.

But for Layla, she would not have it.

Layla's heart had been as cold as ice, and she felt that her brother Dean needed nothing to do with marriage.

For Layla felt that his life had been planned out for him, being single and financially funding the family while she controlled his life, never allowing him to have any happiness outside of her control.

Dean looked at Layla and asked her why she would not congratulate them on their engagement.

Layla refused to give a reason; she continued speaking negative thoughts to Dean. She wanted to instill negative thoughts and the worst outcome in his mind.

A few moments later, Layla continued talking to their mother Rebecca, doing her best to brainwash their mother into thinking that Katie was unkind.

But Rebecca and Katie's bond only grew fonder, and Dean and Katie's love only grew stronger.

Layla refused to give up on her fight to break them apart. Layla was determined to stop the wedding and get Katie far gone.

Dean pleaded with Layla to give Katie a chance.

Dean expressed that all he ever wanted in life was to find someone to love and to love him in return and that he wanted to have a family of his own and to enjoy life.

Dean explained how he would still be there to help with their mother's farm and help the family financially as they needed.

But for Layla, she did not bend to her brother's request, for she felt he did not deserve this happiness.

Layla felt he was to be enslaved to all their family needs, depriving Dean of happiness outside of the family. And he was to stay under her control—never to marry, only date, and stay away from friends.

Katie's heart began to break, seeing the pain in Dean's eyes, which Layla was causing him.

Katie was unsure how to help Dean get through to Layla. She offered her kindness and her friendship, but Layla continued to refuse both.

As the afternoon came to an end and Rebecca had met the children, Dean told his mother they had to be getting back.

Dean, Katie, and the children said their goodbyes and hugged the family.

Layla still refused to show any further kindness to Katie as they said goodbye.

COVID *Virus Outbreak*

As time went on, Katie and Dean continued to plan their wedding and working their careers while raising the children together. They continued helping to care for Katie's parents and Dean's mother.

Katie and Dean had set a date for their wedding, hoping that everything would be perfect and that Layla would warm her cold heart and come around for the sake of her little brother Dean.

As the days were flying by quickly, everyone seemed so busy trying to keep the balance with home and careers.

Dean and Katie continued planning for their wedding when a sudden tragedy hit Katie's family.

Katie was working as a medical administrator when she got the call that instantly broke her heart.

It had been one of her older sisters calling, stating that it was an emergency with her father.

Katie's father had had a heart attack and was rushed to the hospital unconscious. Her sister told Katie that she needed to get to the hospital right away, for they did not think their father would make it.

Katie hurried and rushed to the hospital, tears rolling down her face. She began talking to God, praying her father would make it. She pleaded with God to save him, stating that she loved her father very much and that he was a good man and that her family still needed him here with them.

As Katie finished her prayer, she arrived at the hospital and was greeted by her sister at the emergency room entrance. Her sister's face was swollen from crying; she grabbed Katie and hugged her.

She then led Katie inside the emergency room entrance, where the rest of their family had been seated waiting for answers.

As the doctor came through the emergency room doors, they began speaking to Lauren and Katie's family.

The doctors stated that there was too much damage done to her father's heart and that he was very sorry to tell their family their father was not going to make it.

The doctors continued explaining that they had him on life support and pain medicine to make their father comfortable.

But it was time for the family to go in and say their goodbyes and let him know that they loved him.

Katie screamed, "No, no, no, I cannot lose my father! Please, God, no, don't take him!" As she slowly started to fall to the floor, Katie's older sister caught her.

As Lauren went back with Katie's brothers, Katie waited with her sisters as they comforted one another.

A few moments later, Lauren's sons and Katie's brothers stepped back into the waiting room wiping their tears of sorrow away as Katie and her sisters went back to their father's hospital room to say their goodbyes to their father.

As they entered the room, the sound of the machine beeping made Katie's skin crawl. Seeing her father lifeless on the hospital bed, tubes going throughout his nose and mouth and his body frail, Katie began crying harder. She could not believe this was the last time she would see her loving father.

As Katie went to her father's bedside, she began praying once more.

Katie then told her father she loved him and how much she would miss him. She lightly kissed his head and said her goodbyes as her sisters gathered around him.

Their hearts were broken, and sadness filled the room, for today their family was lost.

Their father had gone to heaven, leaving them to mourn.

As the doctor came in the room, he called time of death for Katie's father.

Katie began praying once more.

As the nurse turned off the machines and led the family out of the room to the waiting area, Katie approached her mother and hugged her tightly.

Katie whispered to her mother, "I don't know what to do. I feel so lost."

Lauren responded with "I know, honey. I do too" as they stood there hugging each other.

A while later, Katie slowly calmed herself and called Dean.

Dean had been at work, and though she did not want to disturb him, she needed him.

When Dean heard the news, he rushed to Katie's side at the hospital.

Dean asked if there was anything he could do.

Katie responded that she just needed him to comfort her and the children for when she told them the sad news.

For her children were remarkably close to their grandfather, this was going to shock them badly.

Dean assured Katie that he would help them get through their great loss.

Dean gave Lauren's children and Katie's siblings his deepest sympathies and told them if he could do anything to let him know.

Lauren thanked Dean for that as Dean hugged her.

Dean's heart had been broken too, for he had a strong bond with Katie's father.

Dean felt as if he had lost his own father.

As the family prepared to leave the hospital, Dean had Katie left her car in the parking lot. He told her they would come back for it later, as she was too upset to drive and that he would take her home and be there for her and her children.

Katie's siblings agreed to take their mother home and stay with her until Katie and her family could meet up with them a little while later.

This gave Katie time to gather her children and break the sad news to them.

As the day continued and the children arrived home from school, Katie gave them the sad news. She then comforted her children by explaining how their grandfather had suffered heart complications and didn't make it.

She told her children with tears in her eyes that their grandfather had gone to heaven.

Katie continued to tell her children that their grandfather loved them very much and that he was proud of all of them.

The children told Dean their grandfather loved him too.

Dean and Katie hugged the children in a group hug tightly, shedding tears of sadness for their great loss.

Lauren later informed Katie and Dean along with the rest of their family of their father's funeral arrangements: that he wanted to be cremated and for his remains to stay with Lauren until her time on earth was up, then to place them next to her at her resting place.

The family respected his wishes and had a service to celebrate his life.

The service was beautiful, and many had gathered to say their goodbyes and pay their respects.

As time continued, Katie and Dean continued to be there for Lauren, helping her through their loss and caring for her needs.

Katie's siblings done what they could to help their mother too.

The family tried to stay strong and close through this challenging time, for it was sudden and a difficult loss for everyone.

During the grieving process, Dean never left Katie's side, except for work and to look after his mother and younger brother.

The loss of Katie's father had taken a toll on Lauren. For she began falling into bad health and could no longer be alone.

Katie and her siblings began taking turns staying with Lauren at her home.

As time went on, Lauren's health continued to worsen, and Katie began to worry more.

Lauren asked Katie and Dean to continue planning their wedding, as it gave her something positive to look forward to.

Though Katie felt that she needed more time to grieve the loss of her father, Lauren assured her it would be best for the family to have something happy to look forward to.

Katie agreed to her mother's wishes and began continuing to plan the wedding.

As the wedding plans were going smoothly, the world was shaken by another tragic event: a virus that was very contagious had broken out and took the lives of many.

The government had called it the COVID virus, whereas others were calling it H1N1 flu.

For many, if they had a weakened immune system or if they were elderly or infants, the virus would hurt them more if they had caught it.

The world was put on lock down, and people were forced to wear face mask if they go in public for work or necessities.

Doctors were overbooked and the same with hospitals and other care facilities.

As no one knew how to treat this, the spread of it was like a forest fire out of control.

The virus would last for a few years, though the world would not know this yet, causing a shortage of food and necessities around the world—once again changing things for everyone, as everyone aimed to survive and beat the virus.

Katie had set her concerns on keeping her mother healthy and safe, all while keeping her children and Dean safe and trying to stay healthy herself.

Dean has done his best to keep his mother healthy and tried to avoid catching the virus.

For if Rebecca and Lauren had caught the virus, they would surely not be able to fight it with their health being in the shape they were in.

Katie prayed for the virus to end, for she did not know what she would do, should her mother catch it.

Katie tried her best to keep her mother safe, making sure her mother stayed indoors.

Lauren had only gone in public for her healthcare appointments.

Katie made sure she wore a mask when she took care of her mother.

Katie made sure to protect her mother when she went outdoors and returned home again.

As time continued, Katie bought her new farm and moved her mother in with her and her children.

Katie felt that she could keep her mother safer and better care for her this way, by having her mother in her home.

As her mother's home was passed down in the family, life became a challenge, but Katie rose to it.

Katie was going to do everything she could to keep everything going smoothly as she could.

With the help of her children, Katie managed to keep a balance in life.

Her children were nearly grown and close to graduating high school.

Losing Katie's Mother

As the COVID virus forever changed the world, it affected many people's health, including Katie's mother.

For early one morning, Lauren had awakened sickly. Her breathing was challenged, and she was dizzy.

Katie had called an ambulance that rushed Lauren to the hospital. For it was the only thing Katie knew to do.

Lauren had a high fever and was extremely sick. Once at the hospital, they admitted Lauren for pneumonia and the COVID virus.

Lauren would stay in the hospital several days.

With the COVID virus still running wild, the hospital would not allow visitors, leaving Lauren without guests to visit or stay.

Katie was so afraid she prayed for her mother to get better.

Katie could not imagine what her mother was going through, for Lauren was older and not used to being alone with strangers.

Katie would call her mother several times a day and send her "get well" flowers.

Once Lauren started feeling better, her doctor stated that they had done test on Lauren and found that she had a weak heart.

The doctor expressed how when an elder loses their life partner, they called it broken heart syndrome.

The doctor expressed that though not medically proven, he felt that Lauren suffered from it and that she would need to get physical therapy to strengthen her body once she beat the COVID virus.

The doctor continued speaking of how Lauren was very weak and would need assistance standing and walking.

Katie took the doctor's words and advice to heart.

For when Lauren beat the COVID virus and was ready to leave the hospital, she had to transfer to short-term care for physical therapy to strengthen her body.

As the time neared for the transfer, everything had gone smoothly. Lauren was transferred to a local clinic close to Katie for short-term care.

Katie was then able to visit her mother through her window and to talk on her cell phone, giving her mother, Lauren, comfort that she was there.

For COVID restrictions, visitors were not allowed to come inside the facility.

As time went on and Lauren began to heal, Katie made plans to bring her mother back home.

Katie made up her mother's room, making sure she would be able to live comfortably.

Katie prepared the family for her mother's homecoming. Everyone was excited, knowing that Lauren was returning home.

As the day approached for Lauren to return home to Katie's care, a call came in that would forever change Katie's world.

It had been the care facility stating that Katie's mother had an encounter with another patient and was exposed to the COVID virus once more and that Lauren had to go into quarantine for another two weeks and could not be released yet.

Katie became terribly upset, for she could not understand how this had happened.

Katie felt the facility knew her mother would be leaving to return home.

Katie could not understand why her mother was not kept separate from the other patients to keep her in good health for her mother, Lauren, to be released into Katie's care.

Katie tried and tried to seek answers to her questions where her mother was concerned.

But Katie's questions went ignored, and though she reached out to higher management, no one would give her a clear explanation for an answer.

Katie waited patiently for the fourteen days to pass by as she continued to visit her mother at the facility through her window.

Though her mother was weak and could not speak, it brought her comfort knowing that her daughter Katie was there.

As time passed and Lauren was about to be released into Katie's care, Katie received another call from her mother's doctor.

Lauren's doctor stated that her mother had taken a turn for the worse overnight and that her mother's body was shutting down. The doctor continued stating that her mother was too weak to continue fighting.

Katie insisted that they rush her mother to the emergency room and get a second opinion.

Katie refused to believe the news she had received.

Though Lauren's doctor disagreed that it was not necessary, he obliged Katie's request and sent her mother to the hospital.

Katie hurried to the hospital to be there upon her mother's arrival.

As the ER doctor examined Lauren, he said she was very frail and immediately transferred her out to a larger hospital, where she could receive better care from specialists.

As Katie and her siblings waited for answers, they prayed for God to save their loving mother.

Though as time went on and with the best care Lauren could receive, Lauren's heart was too weak to continue.

For Katie and her siblings had to say goodbye to their loving mother, for she had been fading fast.

A family was broken, and tears flooded the room, for Lauren was the glue that held the family together.

Lauren's heart was full of love, Her smile could light a room, and her hugs could warm any heart.

But now the family was forever blue.

Lauren had one request for Katie and Dean before her passing. She wanted to see her daughter Katie get married.

Katie wanted to honor her mother's request, so with permission from the facility, the staff at the facility helped Katie and Dean perform a small ceremony at Lauren's beside.

With the help of the facility chaplain, Katie and Dean took their vows and became husband and wife, honoring Katie's mother and giving Lauren her last wish: for Katie and Dean to be married before she passed on to the other side.

Not long after, the doctors told Katie and her family that it would not be much longer that her loving mother would be leaving them.

Katie's heart was broken; she would do anything to save her mother, but it had been out of her hands.

Katie knew her life would be forever changed, for her mother was her best friend and taught her everything.

Katie knew that life would be hard moving forward without her mother.

For without her mother, Katie felt loss.

As Katie was forced to say goodbye to her mother for the last time, tears flooded her eyes.

Katie's knees weakened as she hit the floor next to her mother's hospital bed.

She prayed for her mother and then thanked her mother for the life she gave her and all the love she shared with her.

Katie told her mother she was the best mother she could be blessed with. Then she kissed her mother's cheek one more time as she whispered in her mother's ear she loved her.

A tear rolled down her mother's cheek as Lauren took her final breath and crossed over to the other side.

Katie knew her mother was saying goodbye.

Katie's heart was broken as tears filled her eyes.

The rest of Katie's family came in to say their goodbyes to their mother.

Dean comforted Katie, assuring her that her mother would forever live on in her heart and in the hearts of her children and everyone that loved her and knew her for the beautiful soul she was.

As time went on, Katie and her family continued to grieve and make funeral arrangements for their loving mother.

This had been the hardest day of Katie's and her family's lives.

For to lay your mother to rest was the worse feeling one could experience.

For Katie, it felt as if she had passed on with her mother. Her heart was broken, and she knew not what to do except pray and keep moving forward for her children.

The day came when Lauren was laid to rest; her funeral was beautiful.

Katie honored her mother's wishes and played her favorite songs.

The preacher spoke a lovely sermon for her mother's soul to move on.

Katie and her siblings tried to comfort one another in the best way they knew how.

They all knew that moving forward would be difficult. For no one could ever replace their mother.

As life continued, the days felt forever long, and Katie and her family continued to grieve.

Katie tried to keep her mother's legacy alive and spoke about her often.

Katie wanted to always remember the good times with her mother and all she had taught her.

Katie wanted her children to remember the lessons their grandmother taught them and to remember how much she loved them.

For Katie promised her mother that she would never let anyone forget her. For Lauren was a very special woman, very beautiful with a huge, loving heart.

Layla's Plans of Deceit

Katie and Dean continued with their lives, though still grieving the loss of Katie's mother.

Katie tried to remain strong for her children. She knew her mother would want her to continue living and raise her children to be good-hearted adults one day.

As news got out about Katie and Dean's nuptials, Dean's mother had gotten terribly upset.

Though Dean assured his mother, Rebecca, that he and Katie had planned to renew their vows in the future, they were waiting for the COVID virus to be gone.

Rebecca remained angry, for she felt that it was not necessary to have married so suddenly as they chose to.

Dean assured his mother of the reason for their sudden ceremony.

But Rebecca had been set in her own ways and would not hear of any reason.

With the small dispute between Dean and his mother Rebecca, Layla felt she would use this as an opportunity to drive a wedge between her brother and their mother.

As Layla succeeded with her plan, causing a rift to form between Dean and their mother, Rebecca.

Katie tried to help Dean mend the wedge between him and his mother by reaching out to Rebecca with a heart-to-heart conversation.

Rebecca showed sympathy for Katie with the loss of her mother.

Katie explained once more to Rebecca the reason for her and Dean's sudden wedding ceremony was to honor her mother's last wish, and she assured Rebecca that there would be another ceremony for her and Dean to renew their vows for Rebecca and the rest of Dean's family and friends to attend along with Katie's family and friends.

Rebecca seemed to feel better over this assurance from Katie.

Rebecca began speaking to her son Dean once again with love and kindness.

Rebecca had shared the news with all their family and friends, and though some congratulated them, others were not so excited for them.

Layla felt that she had lost by not getting Katie out of Dean's life, and she did not like losing.

Layla began telling her mother, Rebecca, false truths once more, trying her hardest to tear her mother and Dean apart.

Rebecca became bitter over the words Layla said to her.

Rebecca wanted nothing more than for her children to get along, especially since they were grown adults with families of their own.

However, with the trouble that Layla continued to cause, she had pushed her brother Dean away.

For Dean felt he had been betrayed by his oldest sister. He felt that he had done plenty for his oldest sister over the years.

Dean felt he did not deserve the trouble that Layla was causing him.

Layla continued to speak to Dean's two older sisters and younger brother, trying to drive a wedge between them all.

Layla wanted to start a family war and push Dean farther and farther apart from his family.

As gossip flew between Dean's family members, hearts continued to ache. For their once were a loving, happy family that had welcomed a beautiful new daughter-in-law and new grandchildren had turned into something that Dean no longer recognized.

Dean had never seen this side of his family before.

For Dean's new bride, Katie, had given so much to the family. Katie brought love and joy and celebrated each of them in so many ways.

Katie never asked for anything in return. She only wanted to feel welcomed and loved by them.

Though as time went on, Layla's jealousy slowly broke Dean's family, as Dean's family no longer gathered for celebrations or family dinners.

A few would come to visit Dean and Katie at their new home.

But for Layla, she had turned Rebecca's heart bitter, and she no longer would accept visitors in fear of the unknown.

Katie continued to send her new mother-in-law regular flower deliveries and cards, hoping to assure Rebecca of how much she and Dean and their children loved her and were thinking of her.

Though Rebecca would call and thank Dean and Katie for the lovely flowers and cards, she felt that the wedge brought between Dean and his sister Layla was just too hard.

Rebecca did not know what to do to fix it.

Rebecca assured Layla that no one would ever take her place in her heart.

But for Layla, she allowed envy and greed to change her heart.

Dean assured his mother that he would stay in touch and that he would look out for his brother, should something happen to his mother's health down the road.

Rebecca thanked her son Dean and told him she was proud of him and that she was proud that he found a loving wife.

As Rebecca spoke words of wisdom to Dean, he listened and took her words to heart.

Dean told his mother he loved her dearly and that he was sorry that his sister Layla would not change her heart.

Dean continued telling his mother how Katie felt that she had gained three new sisters with Layla, Skylar, and Journey and a new brother with Carsen and how his stepchildren felt that they gained new aunts and a new uncle.

Rebecca giggled and said that it was great to hear. Though she did not know how to help Dean blend the family smoothly.

Rebecca reassured Dean that sometimes change was just too hard for some people to accept.

Rebecca felt that was the issue with Layla, and she told Dean to continue to pray for her.

Dean listened to his mother's advice and continued to do as she instructed.

Dean reached out to Layla in hopes of fixing the rift that came between them, assuring his big sister that he loved her and that he wanted nothing more than for her and Katie to be friends.

Though for Layla, she continued to harden her heart and felt that Dean marrying was a threat to her inheritance and would not welcome Katie into the family.

Dean called his mother and explained to her how he reached out to his sister Layla, and he told his mother how he pleaded with Layla to stop this family feud.

Dean continued explaining to his mother the unkind words his sister had spoken to him and how his sister ended the conversation with making him feel worthless and broken.

Rebecca reassured Dean that time would heal all wounds and that Dean just needed to give his sister space and pray for a better outcome in the future.

Dean took his mother's words to heart and prayed for a brighter future. He felt time would tell how things would go from there.

Dean felt, from the moment he was living in, that he needed to focus on his new bride and stepchildren and start his new family out on a bright and healthy pathway.

CHAPTER 17

Love Conquers All

As time continued passing by, Dean was determined to stop Layla from destroying their family.

Dean had contacted several members of his family and pleaded for their help. He felt that the love the family shared would be the answer to solving the family feud that Layla had caused.

Dean was able to receive help he needed from multiple members of his family.

Their family bond was strong, and everyone wanted to keep it strong.

Dean's family was proud of him for marrying a loving woman that treated him kindly and loved him with her whole heart.

Dean was an amazing stepfather to Katie's children, and they had grown close as a new family.

As the family was healing from their many losses with the passing of Katie's parents, they wanted nothing more than to cherish the time they had on earth.

Dean's mother had been aging, and the family knew she would not have much time left. Dean hoped for Rebecca to get to know her new grandchildren and daughter-in-law better.

With the world forever changing, things seemed to slowly get back to normal, the normal that everyone was used to.

Dean and Katie were optimistic for their future. They began planning for their vow renewal, in hopes that this would lift Rebecca's spirits and bring everyone closer together.

Though once again, as the date grew near for Dean and Katie's vows renewal, Dean's mother became sick. She had gotten the COVID virus, just as the world thought they had passed it. Rebecca's doctor had admitted her in the hospital.

Devasted, Dean's family prayed for their mother to get through it and to survive it.

They had suffered enough losses already.

As they waited for the time to show the outcome, it felt as if the world stood still.

As Dean and his family began to grow closer, they felt as if their mother's illness was bringing everyone back together.

Dean felt that this was his mother's love working through all of them.

Dean told his siblings that their mother would not have much time left.

After knowing how Katie's mother passed on after catching the COVID virus, Dean told his siblings that the health of Katie's mother was not much different than their own mother's health.

Rebecca's doctor explained to Dean and his family that this was possibly the end for their mother and that they needed to make their peace and express their final words with her to prepare for their mother's passing.

As Dean's family prayed together, knowing that so much time was lost with the feuding between the siblings, they began to realize how short life was.

Dean expressed how painful it was losing Katie's mother, Lauren. He continued expressing to them that Katie was only long-ing to be a part of their family and that Katie wanted nothing more and that she loved them all as family.

Dean continued explaining how Katie had shown their mother and him so much love and how Katie brought back what had been missing for so long: the family gatherings and the laughter they shared together.

Dean continued explaining how the love Katie and her children brought to the family he had not seen in years and that he had seen a light in their mother that she had not shown since the divorce from their father.

Dean's sisters began to shed tears, for they knew the suffering their mother went through when their father had left them.

Dean explained how Katie would do so much for their mother and how Katie would visit her on her days off from her career with the medical clinic.

Dean continued telling his siblings how Kayden would make their mother laugh and joke with their brother and how seeing the children warmed their mother's heart, especially at Christmas, when the children helped her put up her table Christmas tree.

"Oh, how she loved it!" Dean stated.

It was memories like these that Dean would forever hold on to.

As the family acknowledged the memories Dean shared, their hearts began to open. They only wanted to see Dean happy and cherish the moments they had with their mother.

Though Layla was still stuck in her way, Dean could see that his words had touched her heart.

Layla was determined to never change her mind about Katie.

When the moment came, Rebecca's doctor stated that there was no more they could do and that the family needed to say their final goodbyes to their mother.

Dean felt as if he was reliving his nightmare.

For Dean, he was reliving the moment when Katie had to say goodbye to her mother.

As the family took their turns saying their final words to their mother Rebecca, Katie felt her heart breaking all over again.

Watching Dean go through the suffering of losing his mother, Katie felt all she could do was to hold her husband and be there for him.

Katie continued to remind Dean that his mother would live on in his heart, just as Dean reminded Katie that her mother would live on in hers.

Katie told Dean she would be right there beside him and help him grieve his loss, as he did for her when she lost her mother.

As Dean and his family finished speaking their final words to their mother, they said "I love you" one last time and gave their mother a hug goodbye as their eyes filled with tears rolling down their cheeks.

The doctor came in and called the time of death as he turned off the machine.

For Dean's mother had passed, and her spirit had moved on.

The family hugged one another in sadness, knowing that she was no longer suffering in pain.

As time went on and the family grieved, they gave her a beautiful service and laid her to rest in peace.

Dean continued to move on in life not knowing how to handle his grief.

Katie remained right beside him, helping her husband through his grieving.

Katie became his rock and his shoulder to cry on, as she helped her husband every step of the way.

Katie's heart was broken. She had lost her mother and then the passing of her mother-in-law not long after.

Though Katie tried to be strong for Dean, she found herself crying silently in her pillow. For the pain she felt, Katie knew not how to handle. Katie turned to prayer and found her answers. For the Heavenly Father was always there, just like her mother taught her.

Katie assured Dean that God would heal his broken heart and help them through their losses.

Dean found comfort in his faith and knew that Katie stood there beside him.

As time went on, the estate of Dean's mother was handed down to the family.

Dean made sure that his mother's wishes were met.

Dean kept his promise to his mother and looked after his younger brother.

Though for Layla, she remained with hatred in her heart toward Dean, for he saw through her and protected his family and his mother's wishes, keeping Layla from taking everything and making sure his mother's memories lived on with the family and all who loved her.

Dean was still close to his younger brother, along with his sister Journey and Skylar.

Though for Layla, Dean continued to pray for her in hopes that time would change her.

Layla's heart grew colder the day she met Katie.

With that, Layla never gave Katie a chance.

For Layla allowed ugliness to fill her heart.

Layla had hoped that Katie and Dean would not last.

Dean and Katie married and found that true love conquers all.

As life continued, Katie's children grew up and became fine young men. They, too, each found true love and married and began families of their own.

Kayden, Liam, and Cody blessed Katie and Dean with many grandchildren.

Katie continued in her mother's footsteps, helping her children with her grandchildren.

Katie helped her sons with their children—teaching them lessons of life, giving them lots of love and care, and spoiling them, just as Katie's mother had done for her and her siblings when they were young.

Katie and Dean began growing elderly together and lived a long, happy life together. They shared many memories with their grandchildren about their great-grandparents and taught them many skills about life.

Katie and Dean had a love that lasted for them a lifetime, a love that could not be broken by anyone.

To this day, the stories of their bowe live on in their children and grandchildren.

For Katie and Dean loved each other far more than words. They shared their love for God, and they will always be remembered by their family as a love that withheld the storm and got them through anything that came at them.

For they always wanted their children to remember that life is precious and not to be taken for granted and that together, a family's love can build many adventures and loving memories to cherish that last a lifetime.

Like a strong bridge with a strong foundation that will stand forever, love will last forever, being a strong bond. But alone, the world is hard, and it can shatter a sensitive heart and break a loving soul.

THE END

Cheryl Bowyer is a Christian mother of three boys and enjoys spending time with her sons in the great outdoors and traveling. She also loves animals and charitable work. She grew up in a large family, close to her parents and siblings. Cheryl loves creative writing and remodeling/decorating homes and watching Hallmark movies.